Copyright Notice

AWS Certified Solutions Architect Associate

Certification Study Notes (SAA-C01)

Disclaimer

This book was written as a study guide for obtaining AWS certification. While every effort has been made to make this book as accurate as possible no warranty is implied. The author shall not be liable or responsible for any loss or damage arising from the information contained in this book.

About The Author

Shaun Hummel is a Senior Network Engineer with 15+ years of network design, implementation and training experience across national and globally connected infrastructure. He is the author of multiple vendor certification books. The certification training strategy is based on a step-by-step approach with study guides, lab training and practice tests. It is all designed to prepare you for passing the AWS certification exam.

Contents

Contents

Introduction

The technical skills required for information technology is changing rapidly with SDN, network programmability and automation. The virtualization of servers, applications and network devices is causing an overlap of management domains for network, systems and security engineers. The network devices and applications now reside at network servers as virtual machines (VM). In addition there is a shift toward an internet-based connectivity model that is changing how the network is managed. The server-centric architecture redefines how network capacity is managed as well. There are newer virtualized management solutions have been developed for integrating physical and virtual platforms.

Each group must develop new skills for virtualization, server-based troubleshooting and cloud management. The virtualization of applications and devices allow for an on-demand connectivity and operational model. It is characterized by a dynamic, elastic, scalable architecture that is hardware independent. The new networking paradigm uses Open APIs, overlays and SDN programmable network devices. The virtualization overlay abstracts the underlying network infrastructure from the application layer. The virtualization architecture is now enabling seamless access and global connectivity of enterprise and cloud data center applications.

The increasing popularity of cloud computing is the result of its operational model that now has enterprise companies migrating data center applications to cloud facilities. **According to a recent study almost 70% of all IP internet traffic will terminate at a cloud facility by 2018**.

AWS certification has become popular as a training platform for systems administrators, engineers and architects. Candidates must answer technical questions and have the skills required to select, deploy, integrate and maintain AWS cloud solutions. The content for exam study notes is based on official AWS certification guidelines. It covers all exam topics required to pass *AWS Certified Solutions Architect Associate* certification exam.

Study Guide Topics

Domain	Topics
EC2 Compute	AMI, EBS, Auto-Scaling, ElastiCache, ELB, ALB, NLB, EIP, Pricing Models, Instance Types, Resource Tags, Ping
Virtual Private Cloud	Routing Tables, IP Addressing, Subnetting, NAT Instance, Endpoints, Peering, DNS, DHCP, NAT Gateway, Security Groups, ACL, Internet Gateway, Virtual Private Gateway, Direct Connect, VPN
Storage Services	S3, Glacier, AWS Storage Gateway, Snowball, AWS Import/Export, EFS, Consistency Models
Security Architecture	Security Token Service (STS), Identity and Access Management (IAM), Shared Responsibility Model, Best Practices, KMS, Bastion Host, DDoS Mitigation, WAF, SSL/TLS, IDS/IPS, Host-Based Firewall, SAML, Web Identity Federation, Inspector
Database Services	DynamoDB, RDS, MySQL, PostgreSQL, Redshift, EMR, Aurora
Fault Tolerant Systems	DNS Route 53, RTO/RPO, Disaster Recovery Services, Snapshots, Multi-AZ
Deployment/Orchestration	API Gateway, SQS, Kinesis Data Streams, Firehose, Lambda, CORS, CloudFront, Beanstalk, CloudFormation, OpsWorks, Data Pipeline, ECS, Stateless Systems, Loose Coupling
Monitoring Services	CloudWatch, CloudTrail, SSH/RDP, SNS, Flow Logs, Trusted Advisor

AWS Certified Solutions Architect - Associate Exam Guide (SAA)

The following is the AWS Certified Solutions Architect Associate exam guidelines currently published online for reference.

Introduction

The AWS Certified Solutions Architect - Associate (SAA-C01) examination is intended for individuals who perform a Solutions Architect role. This exam validates an examinee's ability to effectively demonstrate knowledge of how to architect and deploy secure and robust applications on AWS technologies.

It validates an examinee's ability to:

- Define a solution using architectural design principles based on customer requirements.

- Provide implementation guidance based on best practices to the organization throughout the lifecycle of the project.

Recommended AWS Knowledge

- One year of hands-on experience designing fault-tolerant, cost-efficient, available and scalable distributed systems on AWS

- Hands-on experience using compute, networking, storage, and database AWS services

- Hands-on experience with AWS deployment and management services

- Ability to identify and define technical requirements for an AWS-based application

- Ability to identify which AWS services meet a given technical requirement

- Knowledge of recommended best practices for building secure and reliable applications on the AWS platform

- An understanding of the basic architectural principles of building on the AWS cloud

- An understanding of the AWS global infrastructure

- An understanding of network technologies as they relate to AWS

- An understanding of security features and tools that AWS provides and how they relate to traditional services

Content Outline

Design Resilient Architectures	34%
Define Performant Architectures	24%
Specify Secure Applications and Architectures	26%
Design Cost-Optimized Architectures	10%
Define Operationally Excellent Architectures	6%

Domain 1: Design Resilient Architectures

1.1 Choose reliable/resilient storage.
1.2 Determine how to design decoupling mechanisms using AWS services.
1.3 Determine how to design a multi-tier architecture solution.
1.4 Determine how to design high availability and/or fault tolerant architectures.

Domain 2: Define Performant Architectures

2.1 Choose performant storage and databases.
2.2 Apply caching to improve performance.
2.3 Design solutions for elasticity and scalability.

Domain 3: Specify Secure Applications and Architectures

3.1 Determine how to secure application tiers.
3.2 Determine how to secure data.
3.3 Define the networking infrastructure for a single VPC application.

Domain 4: Design Cost-Optimized Architectures

4.1 Determine how to design cost-optimized storage.
4.2 Determine how to design cost-optimized compute.

Domain 5: Define Operationally-Excellent Architectures

5.1 Choose design features in solutions that enable operational excellence.

EC2 Compute

EC2 Instances

Scalable resizable compute capacity is provided with Amazon AWS cloud infrastructure. EC2 instance is a virtual server comprised of an operating system, application files and configuration settings that is bundled into an Amazon Machine Image (AMI). EC2 instances are launched from an AMI that serves as a template for each server. The primary operating systems are Linux and Windows based AMI.

Launch EC2 Instances

EC2 instance associated with an AMI is launched from the EC2 console. There are options to launch instances from AWS CLI and AWS Tools for Windows PowerShell as well. EC2 instances must be launched first before access is available with client software.

[EC2 Console]
- Launch instance from launch instance wizard
- Launch instance from a launch template
- Launch from an existing instance
- Launch Linux instance from EBS snapshot
- Launch AMI from AWS Marketplace

- [CLI] Launch instance from AMI

- [Windows PowerShell] Launch instance from AMI

The root device volume for an EC2 instance contains the image used to boot the instance. The store options for root devices include AMI backed by Amazon EC2 instance store or AMI backed by Amazon EBS. The following is a list of steps required to launch an EC2 instance:

1. Select region
2. Select AMI
3. Select root device type
4. Select virtualization type
5. Select instance type
6. Select security group
7. Create a key pair
8. Assign launch permission

The root device type is either EBS-backed AMI or instance-store backed AMI. Instance store is not persistent and slower than the recommended persistent EBS volumes. There is a requirement for EBS storage and EC2 instance to reside in the same availability zone and by extension region. Any persistent storage associated with an EC2 instance is not deleted when the instance is stopped or terminated. Ephemeral and instance store are temporary working storage that is deleted when the instance is stopped. Amazon automatically replicates EBS volumes as well within the same Availability Zone.

Launch permission for an EC2 instance include public, private and explicit. Tenants connect to a Linux-based EC2 instance with SSH protocol. There are some default launch settings imposed by Amazon AWS when connecting primarily for security purposes. The default user account (username) that is permitted login to EC2 instance for Linux is *ec2-user*. The following is a list of default settings for a Linux AMI based EC2 instance.

- password authentication is disabled
- key pairs are required
- root login is disabled

Access EC2 Instances

Amazon AWS has three primary methods that allow tenants to manage, configure and launch EC2 instances. They include AWS management console, command line interface (CLI) and API programmatic calls. EC2 instances are accessed remotely with management protocols. The client protocol supported for Linux is SSH with terminal emulation software such as PuTTY. In addition there are Windows-based instances accessed and managed with RDP.

Operational Considerations

EC2 instances that are stopped or paused still incur some costs from AWS. You would stop your instance first before terminating to backup your data. That would include instance store to S3 or an EBS volume snapshot. The AMI is then deregistered to prevent launch and instance is terminated to stop billing. Amazon recommends consolidated billing to enable tracking multiple cost centers and volume price discounts.

The following are common reasons for stop and restart of an EC2 instance:

- system status check failed

- scale up/down instance type

- application problems

- modify IP addressing

- backup data

It is not possible for a tenant to restart or connect to an EC2 instance after it has been terminated. The options are to launch a new instance using the same AMI associated with the instance or launch from an EBS snapshot previously made from the volume.

The following occurs when an EC2 instance is terminated:

- Elastic IP removed from network interfaces
- EBS root device volume and any data volumes are deleted
- AWS billing is stopped

There is an error message generated to the management console when an EC2 instance is terminated immediately on launch. Some typical causes include EC2 instances or EBS volume limits exceeded on AWS account. Specific limits that are exceeded will cause any new EC2 instances to terminate. The following are common causes that could prevent EC2 instances from launching.

- security group and/or network ACL is blocking traffic
- launch permission do not exist for AWS user
- private key file name and key pair name do not match
- AWS account limits are exceeded

Termination Protection

Tenants can enable termination protection for an EC2 instance to prevent accidental termination from console, CLI or API. The termination protection is disabled by default. The *DisableApiTermination* attribute when changed to (true) enables termination protection. This feature is available for both Amazon EC2 instance store-backed (S3) and Amazon EBS-backed instances. There is no support for enabling termination protection on Spot instances. The Spot pricing model gives a two-minute warning before terminating an instance however.

Tenant Responsibility

The tenant is responsible for configuring the guest operating system and all application level settings including database structures and associated security access. That would include any security groups and ACLs assigned to a VPC. In addition any virtual appliances deployed to the VPC are configured by tenants based on their requirements.

The configuration settings become part of the AMI bundle created for each EC2 instance. Amazon AWS creates the instances and configures the operating system for managed services such as RDS. EC2 instances including NAT instance are managed by the tenant.

Software maintenance, security updates, managing instance failures and security group rules are the responsibility of tenants. Managing the underlying hosts for RDS and Beanstalk is the responsibility of AWS.

EBS Volume Encryption

It is common to migrate an unencrypted EBS volume to an EBS encrypted volume. The tenant first creates a new EBS encrypted volume of the same size as unencrypted volume. In addition the new encrypted volume is assigned to the same Availability Zone and encryption option is enabled. The convertor instance is started. The unencrypted EBS volume is shutdown and detached before starting data migration between volumes.

EC2 Status Checks

Status monitoring is used to detect any problems that could prevent EC2 instances from running applications properly. EC2 performs automated checks on every running EC2 instance to identify hardware and software issues.

- status checks are every minute and each returns a pass or a fail status
- the overall status of the instance is OK when all checks pass
- the overall status is Impaired when one or more checks fail
- status checks are built into EC2 and cannot be disabled or deleted
- alarms can be created based on the result of the status checks

Customers can either wait for AWS support to fix the system status check fail or resolve it by stopping and restarting or terminating and replacing an EC2 instance. The following are typical causes of system status checks failure.

- loss of network connectivity
- loss of system power
- software issues on the physical host
- hardware issues on the physical host

Amazon Machine Image (AMI)

The EC2 instance is launched from an AMI that serves as a template for each virtual server instance. The primary operating systems are Linux and Windows based AMI. The following describe the primary components of an Amazon AMI.

- Template for the root volume of an EC2 instance with operating system, application and configuration settings.

- Launch permissions that specify AWS account/s that are allowed to launch EC2 instances from that AMI.

- Block device mapping is the configuration for attaching data volumes/s to an EC2 instance when it is launched. There is support for EBS volumes and instance store volumes.

Anytime you make configuration changes to an EC2 instance they only exist for that EC2 instance. Launching new EC2 instances from the same AMI will have the old configuration. The tenant must create a new AMI from the updated EC2 instance that can be used for launching additional instances with the desired settings. The changes could include a variety of settings including adding tags for instance.

Figure 1 EC2 Instance Contents for EBS-backed Linux AMI

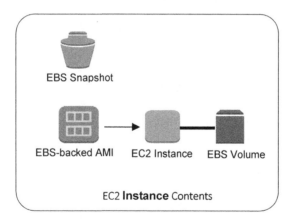

AMI Lifecycle

The following illustrates the lifecycle of an AMI from creating, registering and launching EC2 instances. In addition the AMI can be copied or deregistered to prevent launch of instances. The AWS user must have permissions to perform any of the administrative tasks. Tenants can use *CreateImage* API to create and register an EBS-backed AMI.

Figure 2 Amazon AMI Lifecycle Activities

Create AMI → *Register AMI* → *Launch EC2 Instance*

→ *Copy AMI*

→ *Deregister AMI*

Anytime you make a copy of an AMI it is the instance configuration only and does not include any session data. The Snapshot includes the EBS root volume (for boot) and all EBS data volumes for the instance. That creates an AMI with instances that can boot (launch) and have all data volumes attached.

Copy Snapshot

The tenant would take a Snapshot of the EBS-backed AMI and select *Copy SnapShot* option where destination region is specified. Launching database instances from that AMI would include all session data up to the point on time when the Snapshot was taken. The same is true for a Snapshot of an AMI comprised of a web server EC2 instance.

Create Snapshot of EBS-backed AMI → *Copy Snapshot* → *Select Region*

Amazon AWS does not permit copy of an EC2 instance within or cross-region. It does however allow copying the AMI associated with the EC2 instance. The tenant would select the AMI and then Copy AMI option where destination region is specified. That would make the AMI available in the destination region to launch the EC2 instance. Any launch permissions, user-defined tags or S3 bucket permissions are not copied from the source AMI to the new AMI.

This illustrates a key aspect of launching an AMI vs launching an AMI backed by EBS volume Snapshot. The EC2 instance type determines whether the AMI is instance store-backed (S3) or EBS backed volume. You can select to encrypt the Snapshot with the default keys or specify a custom key.

On-Premises Server Migration

There are VMware tools that convert an on-premises physical server to virtual machine (VM). Amazon AWS Server Migration Server (SMS) automates and replicates the VM server volume and saves it as an AMI image.

The AMI can be used to launch an EC2 instance of a server. In addition the AMI can be used to launch multiple EC2 instances such as web servers for and Auto-Scaling group to increase compute capacity. There is currently no support for converting non-VMware virtual machines using SMS.

Figure 3 Options for Creating an Amazon AWS AMI

Configure EC2 instance → Create AMI → Launch EC2 instance

EBS snapshot → Create AMI → Launch EC2 instance

Select AMI → Launch EC2 instance → Configure → Create new AMI

Instance Types

The tenant selects and assigns an Amazon EC2 instance type to an EC2 instance based on requirements. The capacity planning paradigm shifts somewhat now that the underlying throughput is based on server hardware. Traditional network capacity is based on physical network devices. Cloud virtual appliances and servers are converted to EC2 instances (virtual machines). The cloud provider defines multiple instance types that customers can assign to each server or virtual appliance. Some virtual appliances only support specific EC2 instance types and maximum throughput licensing.

Hardware and Capacity

EC2 instance types are selected based on the application being deployed and specific capacity requirements. The characteristics of an EC2 instance include compute, storage, memory and networking features. In addition there are limitations such as VPC only launch, EBS only volumes and virtualization type. The hardware capacity and features vary for each instance type. The standard features include number of vCPU cores, memory (GB), storage (SSD), throughput and number of network interfaces.

Instance types are either based on instance store or EBS volume storage. In addition there are storage optimized instance types for attached EBS volumes. That allows for increased IOPS and interface throughput. Amazon has an enhanced networking feature as well that are available with some instance types. It provides increased throughput in addition to lower latency and jitter.

Enhanced Networking

The advantages of enhanced networking include higher packet per second (PPS) performance, lower jitter and lower latency for applications. It is based on an optimized virtualization stack with high I/O performance and lower CPU utilization. The tenant must launch an HVM AMI with the correct drivers and assign a supported instance type. The supported instance types provide the Elastic Network Adapter (ENA) interface with *ena* Linux driver. There is no added cost other than instance type and HVM virtualization charges.

Supported Instance Types - C3, C4, C5, D2, I3, I2, H1, M5, M4, X1, R3

Virtualization Type

Current generation instance types all support HVM virtualization type however only C3 and M3 support PV virtualization type as well. The advantages of HVM include enhanced networking support with hardware extensions and hardware virtualization. The hardware extensions provide optimize performance for instances. The hardware virtualization (isolation) enables migration of EC2 instances across various hardware platforms. That permits instances to run operating systems on different hardware platforms without modifications.

Compute optimized EC2 instances types are recommended for data analytics and any processing intensive applications. There are subgroups of compute optimized instances as well that are designed for specific types of applications. Database servers are tables that contain large amounts of data for query and analysis. They require memory optimized instances considering the fact that they increase over time as well.

Auto Scaling

Auto Scaling feature allows the tenant to seamlessly increase aggregate server capacity based on throughput requirements. It is a horizontal scaling of capacity to a server group based on performance thresholds. The number of EC2 instances assigned to an Auto Scaling group increase or decrease based on any exceeded thresholds. It is a service designed specifically for front-end EC2 instances and not database instances.

Basic monitoring is enabled when you create a launch configuration using the AWS Management Console. Detailed monitoring is enabled when you create a launch configuration using the AWS CLI or an API call. CloudWatch cannot notify an Auto Scaling group to scale out.

Scaling Options

Auto Scaling groups are defined with an initial number of EC2 instances that enable horizontal scaling. The scaling policy is used to increase or decrease the number of EC2 instances for a group based on utilization (workload). Capacity is managed dynamically by adding instances (scaling out) or removing instances (scaling in) from an Auto-Scaling group. There are several different options that affect how scaling can be deployed for an Auto Scaling group.

1. Maintain current instance levels

Scaling is based on maintaining a minimum or specified number of running instances at all times. Any unhealthy instances detected by health check are terminated and replaced with a new instance.

2. Manual scaling

Scaling is based on change in the maximum, minimum or desired capacity of an Auto Scaling group. Creating or terminating instances to maintain the updated capacity is managed by Auto Scaling.

3. Schedule

Scaling actions are performed automatically based on a configured time and date when known capacity increases and/or decrease will occur.

4. Scaling policy

Scaling policy define operational parameters such as performance conditions, workload or operational status. Amazon AWS recommends a separate scaling in policy for terminating instances and scaling out policy for launching instances.

The scaling in policy would remove a specified number of instances for example when bandwidth utilization drops below a specific threshold. In addition scaling out policy would launch a certain number of instances when workload increases. CloudWatch alarm are used to trigger scale in and scale out capacity for an Auto-Scaling group policy.

Auto Scaling Group

All EC2 instances are launched from a single AMI for the same server group (web server for example). The private IP addressing is automatically assigned to instances from a DHCP server. In addition the tenant cannot explicitly assign EIP or network ACL from a launch configuration. The options for creating an Auto Scaling group include launch template, launch configuration or EC2 instance (manual). The launch template creates an auto launch configuration that allow multiple versions with different launch configuration settings. The configuration attributes include AMI ID, instance type, key pair, security group/s and block device mapping.

Termination Policy

The termination policy is configured to select what instance is terminated first when automatic scaling in is enabled for an Auto-Scaling group. AWS instance protection is available as well to prevent Auto Scaling from selecting specific instances for termination when scaling in. Default termination policy is designed to ensure instances are distributed evenly across multiple Availability Zones.

When using the default termination policy, Auto Scaling selects an instance to terminate based on two conditions initially. The Availability Zone (AZ) with the most instances and where at least one instance is not protected from scale in. Where there is a tie, it is an unprotected instance with oldest launch configuration terminated.

Classic Load Balancer

EC2 elastic architecture optimizes availability and provides on-demand capacity to tenants. Amazon AWS Elastic Load Balancer (ELB) automatically distributes inbound application traffic from the internet across single or multiple Availability Zones and Auto-Scaling groups. Amazon AWS provides classic, application and network load balancer types that are each deployed based on requirements. They enable automatic scaling and fault tolerance for cloud applications.

Classic Load Balancer is Layer 4 connection-oriented where incoming requests are equally distributed across multiple instances for a single application only. There is support for TCP and SSL listeners not available with an Application Load Balancer. Amazon AWS recommends that tenants deploy the same number of EC2 instances per load balancing group in each Availability Zone.

EC2 instances are authenticated to Classic Load Balancer with a public key. The load balancer only communicates with an EC2 instance when the public keys match. In addition SSL and security certificates are supported for in-transit data security.

Register EC2 Instances

Elastic Load Balancer (ELB) is attached to a single or multiple Auto Scaling groups with EC2 instances. ELB automatically registers the instances and distributes incoming traffic from the internet across all available EC2 instances. EC2 instances must be registered manually to an ELB if the instances were launched during a suspension period.

ELB enters the *Adding* state while registering the instances in the group and then it enters the *Added* state. The ELB enters *InService* state after at least one registered instance passes the health checks . Auto-Scaling does not terminate and replace EC2 instances unless ELB enters *InService* state. EC2 instances that are deregistered from an ELB remain running however they receive no traffic. ELB connection draining is a feature that when enabled allows in-flight requests to complete before the EC2 instance is deregistered.

Health Checks

Elastic Load Balancer routes requests to the active EC2 instance with the lowest utilization as a default setting. ELB automatically reroutes the traffic to the remaining running healthy EC2 instances when an instance fails. ELB Controller service stores the configuration and scales up/down capacity of the load balancer for incoming requests. The controller service scales the load balancer to handle more connections and requests, scaling equally in all zones.

ELB monitors server health and failover user sessions to available servers. That would include load balancing servers across Availability Zones at redundant data centers. Elastic Load Balancers runs health checks to detect when web server EC2 instances are unavailable or over-utilized. It is the Auto-Scaling group that is notified and replaces the EC2 instance. The advantage of ELB health check is that it provides application level status.

The default health check for an Elastic Load Balancer is to open a TCP connection to the EC2 instance. The instance is moved to unhealthy state if the load balancer cannot connect within the timeout interval. The following occurs when an EC2 instance fails health check.

- Auto-scaling group removes the instance
- ELB no longer forwards traffic to that instance

Configuration Steps

The following is a list of steps required to configure Classic Load Balancer: There is support for SSL termination that offloads SSL processing from EC2 instances to Elastic Load Balancer as well. Tenants must add an SSL certificate and configure HTTPS as a listener for encrypted sessions.

Step 1: Select a load balancer type

Step 2: Define your load balancer

Step 3: Assign security group to load balancer in a VPC

Step 4: Configure health checks for your EC2 instances

Step 5: Register EC2 instances with your load balancer

Step 6: Tag your load balancer (optional)

Step 7: Create and verify your load balancer

ELB Operation

The client connection starts with making a DNS request to resolve the IP address assigned to an Elastic Load Balancer. AWS advertises the DNS name of each Elastic Load Balancer to the internet. The Amazon DNS servers resolve the IP address and return that to the client.

EC2 instances, ELB and Auto-Scaling groups are all deployed to a single Availability Zone by default. AWS recommends you deploy them across multiple Availability Zones for redundancy and horizontal scaling. Amazon automatically enables Multi-AZ for services such as DynamoDB, RDS, S3 and SNS.

Elastic Load Balancer distributes traffic within a single VPC **only** to provide scalability and redundancy for applications. There is cross-region load balancing to multiple ELB that is available when deployed in concert with DNS Route 53. ELB is assigned to the same public subnet as the NAT Gateway and by extension same custom route table. Outbound traffic from the web servers is first forwarded to ELB internal (private address). Each instance is assigned a private IP address for internal VPC routing as a minimum requirement.

Availability Zones/Subnets

There is a load balancer node created in each of the Availability Zone where at least one subnet is configured. ELB is not a router and as a result only one subnet can be attached per Availability Zone to the ELB. Adding a new subnet would replace any existing subnet. The subnet CIDR block must be at least /27 length and a minimum of eight free IP addresses. The subnet can span Availability Zones and recommended for fault tolerance

Tenants connect to EC2 instances assigned to an Auto-Scaling group based on DNS name of the Elastic Load Balancer. The ELB is assigned to a public subnet with a custom route table that has a default route to the Internet gateway. Traffic ingress from the internet is forwarded to the primary private IP address (eth0 interface) of each EC2 instance.

Cross-Zone Load Balancing

There is cross-zone load balancing support as well where the ELB distributes requests to Auto-Scaling groups in different Availability Zones. There is support for load balancing EC2 instances assigned to public and/or private subnets.

Figure 4 Elastic Load Balancer and Cross-Zone Auto-Scaling Groups

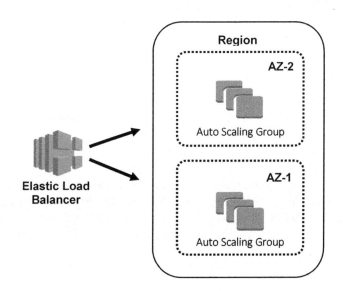

The default setting for cross-zone load balancing is determined by how the classic load balancer is created. For example cross-zone load balancing is disabled by default when enabled from API call or CLI. As a result each load balancer node distributes requests evenly across the registered instances within its assigned Availability Zone only.

The option to enable cross-zone load balancing is selected by default when configuring Classic Load Balancer from AWS Management Console. As a result requests are distributed evenly across the registered instances in all enabled Availability Zones. There is minimal effect on performance when an EC2 instance is removed or the need to maintain equal numbers of EC2 instances in each Availability Zone. AWS does however recommend assigning the same number of instances for best results.

Web-Based Applications

Amazon AWS EC2 instances deployed as web servers (front end tier) support ELB and Auto-Scaling groups as a standard design solution. They provide horizontal scaling for elastic capacity and changing workloads. The minimum requirements are EC2 instances for front end web servers, ELB to distribute requests across multiple instances and Auto-Scaling for fault tolerance. In addition there is S3 multi-purpose storage typically attached. IAM security permissions and CloudWatch monitoring are configured as well. There is CloudFront as an alternative when customers are multi-region (global).

Capacity Pre-Warming

ELB is designed under normal conditions to process gradual workload increases and scale up accordingly. AWS support can *pre-warm* the load balancer upon request. The idea is to configure the load balancer with a sufficient level of capacity based on expected peak traffic events. AWS would require start and end dates in addition to the expected request rate per second with the total size of request/response.

Application and Classic Load Balancers have listeners that define the protocol and port, where the load balancer listens for incoming connections. Each load balancer must have at least one listener with support for ten listeners. Routing rules for path-based routing are defined on listeners along with targets and target groups. Classic Load Balancers support HTTP, HTTPS, TCP and SSL protocols from clients while Application Load Balancers only HTTP and HTTPS.

Security Rules

Configure security groups and network ACL for your internet-facing (default) load balancer to communicate with registered EC2 instances. The internet facing load balancer requires a rule for security group and NACL to permit all TCP inbound traffic on the load balancer listener port from clients.

In addition add an outbound rule that allows traffic to instances on the health check port and instance listener port. NACLs should allow responses on the ephemeral ports for inbound and outbound traffic as well.

Configure security groups and network ACL (NACL) for your internal load balancer. They are not directly connected to the internet (private). That load balancer requires a rule for security group and NACL to permit all TCP inbound traffic from the VPC CIDR subnet range on the load balancer listener port. In addition add an outbound rule that allows traffic to instances on the health check port and instance listener port. NACLs should allow responses on the ephemeral ports for inbound and outbound traffic as well.

CloudWatch Logs

AWS require explicitly enabling logging and configuring IAM role permissions to publish the logs to CloudWatch Log group. The service is called CloudWatch Logs where they are centralized. Elastic Load Balancer when enabled, publishes data to an access log at 5-minute intervals. That includes each request to the load balancer with source IP address and server response. Log files for AWS services are stored in an S3 bucket and where enabled published to CloudWatch Logs. Tenant must grant each AWS services write (PutObject) permission to the S3 bucket.

Application Load Balancer

Application Load Balancer (ALB) enables support to Layer 7 of the OSI model. It provided content-based routing and load balance based on inspection of HTTPS headers. It is well suited to ECS container services as well. ALB can load balance multiple requests to a single or multiple containers that are each comprised of multiple applications. In addition tenants can enable Web Application Firewall (WAF) for security purposes and IPv6 interfaces.

The traditional load balancer HTTP listener rules are based on content with 1:1 application port mapping. Each application is assigned an application port for such routing purposes. AWS now supports assigning unused ports for requests with dynamic port mapping. That allows tenants to run multiple copies of the same task on the same container host (EC2 instance). AWS deploys cluster management to create clusters and assigns EC2 instances for launching containers based on tenant requirements.

Application Load Balancer (ALB) is a managed service that can load balance up to ten different applications per ALB. The ALB is scaled automatically as traffic workload increases. It terminates incoming connections, examines the HTTP header and forwards packets based on a rule set. It acts as a proxy where packet rewrite occurs on the ALB.

HTTP header contains an *X-forwarded-for* field with the client IP address. In addition Application Load Balancer supports path-based routing and dynamic port mapping. The purpose of dynamic port mapping is to route multiple tasks per service to a single container instance.

Table 1 Feature Comparison for Elastic Load Balancer Types

Feature	Classic LB	Application LB	Network LB
Protocols	TCP, HTTP, HTTPS, SSL	HTTP, HTTPS	TCP
Platform	EC2-Classic, VPC	VPC	VPC
Health checks	X	X	X
Connection draining	X	X	X
Cross-Zone load balance	X	X	X
Sticky sessions	X	X	
SSL offload	X	X	
CloudWatch metrics	X	X	X
Access logs	X	X	X
Idle connection timeout	X	X	
Backend encryption	X	X	
Backend authentication	X		
Websockets support		X	X
Path-based routing		X	
Host-based routing		X	
Elastic IP address			X
Static IP address			X
Dynamic port mapping		X	X
IP address as target		X	X
Zonal failover	X	X	X

* Network Load Balancers support IP address targets including outside of the VPC. In addition there is support for containers and dynamic port mapping. In addition there is additional scalability to millions of requests per second. There is support for EC2 instances (web servers), containers and IP addresses as targets.

Amazon AWS provides path-based routing feature with Application Load Balancer (ALB). The purpose is to enable load balancing among multiple applications with a single ALB. The inbound request is routed to an individual application (and member EC2 instance) based on the URL matching a listener rule. The URL refers to a domain and web page used for distinguishing applications and member EC2 instances.

Pricing Models

Amazon AWS pricing models are distinguished based on reliability and discounts. They provide capacity (compute + storage + network) and service levels for a variety of application requirements. Demand model is based on a standard hourly usage, pay as you go, guaranteed access with no service interruption. It is recommended for short term bursty traffic requiring the same on-demand capacity as on-premises applications.

Reserved mode provides up to 75% discounted pricing over demand model however not guaranteed to launch. It is based on availability and cloud traffic loads at that time. Assigning your instance to a specific Availability Zone provides some assurance of instance launch when required. It is recommended for applications where usage time and capacity are known.

Spot model provides up to 90% discount over demand model and based on any excess capacity that is available from Amazon when the instance is launched. The EC2 instances can be interrupted when required for on-demand usage tenant traffic. It is recommended for application profiles such as software development and testing, analytics, batch processing, fault tolerant failover activities and any processing that can be interrupted.

There is no charge when an EC2 instance is stopped. There is however a charge for EBS volume storage unless the instance is terminated. The running instance is charged for a minimum of one minute and then pro-rated in seconds when it is restarted. Data transfer IN to EC2 from the internet is free. Data transfer OUT from EC2 to storage, database and Redshift services is free. The first GB only of data transfer from EC2 OUT to the internet is free.

Resource Tags

EC2 instance supports resource tags that are text strings with a key and optional value. The purpose is to categorize AWS resources by purpose, owner or environment. For example you could assign key = *testops*, value = *testsrv* to identify owner and project instance is assigned.

You can edit tag keys and values, remove tags and set the value of a tag to an empty string however null value is not supported. Adding a tag with the same key as an existing tag to an AWS resource, the new value overwrites the old value. Tags are all deleted when a resource is deleted. The following are AWS resources that do not support tags.

- VPC endpoint
- VPC endpoint service
- VPC flow log
- Reserved Instance listing
- Placement group
- Launch template version
- Key pair
- Egress-only internet gateway
- Dedicated host
- Egress-only internet gateway

Placement Groups

The purpose of an EC2 placement group is to enable higher performance. EC2 instances are launched as a cluster for proximity within the same Availability Zone. As a result placement groups cannot span Availability Zones. There is higher network throughput (10 Gbps) and lower latency for AWS-based applications within the same VPC or peering VPC's.

Select instance types that support enhanced networking feature and 10 Gbps throughput. In addition assigning the same instance type to all instances within the same group is recommended. The architecture of placement groups limit horizontal scaling. Launch all EC2 instances at the same time and number required to avoid insufficient capacity errors. The capacity is allocated at launch time for the placement group. Adding new instances to the group could cause a capacity error. Tenants should stop the group, add new instances and then restart to have additional capacity allocated.

Virtual Private Cloud

VPC Routing

Amazon Virtual Private Cloud (VPC) is an architecture that enables tenants to create a logically isolated segment within the AWS Cloud. The purpose is to provide tenants with maximum control within the cloud environment for its applications. The tenant can duplicate an on-premises network design to the cloud with subnetting, virtual appliances and hybrid cloud connectivity.

There is support for multiple subnet models, complex security and integration with on-premises applications. VPC is a key feature that permits companies to deploy private applications with security compliance requirements. Any single VPC must reside within the same region and subnets cannot span multiple availability zones. There is support for a single VPC or multiple VPC spanning multiple Availability Zones. EC2 instances are launched into an existing VPC based on the VPC name selected. In addition tenants can assign a subnet to the EC2 instance for launch or use default subnetting.

Amazon VPC Router

VPC router is the AWS native router assigned to each VPC that routes packets between subnets within the same VPC and peering VPC connections. Any packets destined for the internet are forwarded to the Internet gateway. In addition the VPC router is used for communicating between subnets, NAT, Internet gateway and virtual private gateway (VPG) when deployed.

The local route is used for communicating between instances within the same subnet only. Any communication between subnets requires the native VPC router. Forwarding packets between private and public subnets requires NAT. The local route is the top level CIDR subnet that is used to create subnets for the VPC. It varies based on whether it is a default VPC (default subnet 172.31.0.0/16), VPC created by the VPC wizard (10.0.0.0/16) or tenant custom addressing. There is a local route installed in the main route table and each custom route table.

Main Route Table

The VPC creates a main route table as the default table. The tenant can then reassign the subnet to a custom route table based on routing requirements. The main route table cannot be deleted and can be assigned to private or public subnets. The same subnet cannot be assigned to more than one route table. Any new subnet created after defining the VPC is associated with the main route table. It has a local route that is used for routing between subnets within a single VPC.

The main route table is typically used for private subnets however the tenant could deploy a single public subnet with web servers for example. The tenant would have to assign an EIP address to each instance for advertising to the internet. The main route table has a default route (0.0.0.0/0) to the Internet gateway automatically if it is created with default VPC option.

Custom Route Table

The custom route table has a local route that is used for routing between subnets as well. In addition the tenant would add a default route to the Internet gateway. The tenant can associate a single or multiple subnets to the same custom route table. The best practice is to move all subnets that require internet access to a custom route table. The tenant must create a custom route table and associate the new public subnet to it. That will move the public subnet from the main route table and advertise the servers assigned to that subnet across the internet. That allows for control of VPC routing and optimizes security.

Network Interfaces

When launching an instance into a VPC, you can optionally assign a primary private IP address from the IPv4 address range of the subnet or AWS will assign it from the configured CIDR block. The private address is assigned to the default network interface (eth0) of the instance. You can add multiple secondary private IP addresses that are often used for virtual appliances. EC2 instances must be terminated to reassign an Elastic IP address to a new EC2 instance.

Elastic Network Interface (ENI)

Elastic Network Interfaces are virtual network interfaces assigned to an EC2 instance within a VPC. ENI supports multiple private IP addresses assignable per network interface. In addition tenants can assign a single public IPv4 address or public Elastic IP to the same interface. In the context of VPC architecture, EC2 instances could include servers or virtual appliances. ENI supports multiple IPv6 addresses, security groups, MAC address and source/destination check attribute.

Elastic IP (EIP)

The public Elastic IP address (EIP) is assigned to a network interface and advertised across the internet. The EIP is a static public address that is persistent (remains assigned) even when the instance is stopped. The support for private and public addressing allows for subnetting and security zones The tenant is assigned a maximum of five static Elastic IP (EIP) addresses per region. There are often multiple public web servers deployed across availability zones. Tenants can enable NAT to conserve addresses or request some additional EIP addresses from Amazon AWS.

Elastic IP vs Public IPv4 Address

Public IPv4 addresses are not persistent or reassignable to a different EC2 instance or interface. Amazon AWS returns public IPv4 addresses to a shared pool when an EC2 instance is stopped. Any assigned private IP addressing is persistent however. EIP is released from an EC2 instance when it is terminated.

EIP is a static internet routable IP address that is persistent when an EC2 instance is stopped. It can be manually reassigned to another instance when there is an instance failure or stopped. There is a nominal charge for EIP while an EC2 instance is stopped. Amazon automatically assigns a public IPv4 address to an instance network interface when the tenant disassociates an EIP from it. In addition the public IPv4 address is released when an EIP is assigned to the network interface

Elastic IP addresses are statically assigned to an AWS tenant account in contrast to public IPv4 addresses that are allocated from a pool. The primary private IP address assigned to each instance cannot be reassigned. They are assignable with DHCP can be manually assigned.

VPC Platforms

The VPC console permits tenants to select either a default VPC or nondefault VPC. Amazon AWS will then programmatically configure and deploy the VPC based on what platform was selected. Refer to Table 2 where there is a feature comparison for each platform. EC2-Classic is still supported for customers that deployed it before 2013.

Default VPC

The default VPC type is a starting point for tenants that enable basic services including internet access. It is now possible to create a default VPC from the AWS management console or CLI. EC2 instances are initially assigned a public IPv4 address (not EIP) and a private IPv4 address. VPC instances support multiple Elastic Network Interfaces (ENI) where each ENI can be configured with a private and/or public IP address. There is a default route (0.0.0.0/0) added to the main route table that forwards packets to the Internet Gateway.

AWS creates a default subnet in each Availability Zone (AZ) of the region where your VPC is located when default VPC type is selected. EC2 instances however are not automatically replicated to each Availability Zone. In addition there is an Internet gateway added for internet access. EC2 instances automatically receive public IPv4 addresses for internet access. Amazon AWS assigns VPC CIDR block 172.31.0.0/16 to your VPC when the default VPC type is selected. It further subnets your VPC with 172.31.0.0/20 addressing for EC2 instances.

That subnets the third octet so that adding four new subnets on the bottom end of the range would include for instance 172.31.0.0/20, 172.31.16.0/20, 172.31.32.0/20 and 172.31.48.0/20 subnets.

The first ten instances assigned to the first subnet (172.31.0.0/20) for example could be assigned 172.31.0.1/20 - 172.31.0.10/20 address range. The tenant would typically assign instances to multiple subnets based on network design, security and application requirements.

The main route table has 172.31.0.0/16 as a local route added as well. There is a default security group that permits all traffic inbound and outbound. By default Amazon selects an Availability Zone and launches the EC2 instance into the subnet associated with that Availability Zone. That only occurs when the tenant launches an EC2 instance without specifying a subnet.

There is a default security group and network ACL associated with default VPC type as well. EC2 instances launched in the default VPC are assigned to the default security group. The tenant can modify any default configuration and create up to 100 security groups per VPC. Traffic into the subnet is filtered with the network ACL. The default security group and network ACL permit all traffic.

Nondefault VPC

The primary reason for selecting nondefault VPC type is to configure all customized settings for your VPC. There are no gateways attached to the VPC unless explicitly enabled. By default, EC2 instances launched into a nondefault VPC are not assigned a public IPv4 address or public DNS hostname. It permits you to configure a customized environment and enable internet connectivity at some point if required.

When an instance is launched into nondefault VPC, each instance is provided a private DNS hostname from Amazon AWS. In addition a public DNS hostname is provided only when DNS hostnames attribute is changed from **no** to **yes** and your instance is using a public IPv4 address.

Customized VPC CIDR Block

The maximum CIDR block range supported for IPv4 addressing within any single VPC is /16 to /28 subnet mask. That would for instance include 10.0.0.0/16 to 10.0.0.0/28 CIDR block range for that private subnet addressing selected. Host routes are configured with /32 subnet mask and is not a subnet.

Tenants often select 10.0.0.0 private addressing as a result of its popularity and deployment for on-premises addressing. For example consider VPC CIDR block of 10.0.0.0/16 and Subnet CIDR block 10.0.0.0/24 (derived from VPC CIDR block) for creating multiple subnets.

Table 2 Feature Comparison for AWS VPC Platforms

Feature	EC2-Classic	Default VPC	Nondefault VPC
Public IPv4 address	instance receives public IP address	assigned on startup as default	not assigned
Private IP address	single private IP address from EC-Classic range (not persistent)	single private IP address range from default range (static)	single private IP address from nondefault range (static)
Multiple private IP addresses	not supported	yes per interface	yes per instance
Elastic IP address	removed from EC2 instance when stopped	persistent with EC2 instance when stopped	persistent with EC2 instance when stopped
DNS hostnames	enabled	enabled	disabled
Security groups	500 per region for multiple AWS accounts	500 groups per VPC assignable to VPC only	500 groups per VPC assignable to VPC only
Security group association	unlimited groups per instance and cannot change while running	5 groups per instance and can change groups while running	5 groups per instance and can change groups while running
Security group rules	100 rules per group and inbound only	50 rules per group for inbound and outbound traffic	50 rules per group for inbound and outbound traffic
Network ACL	inbound only	default ACL	not assigned
Hardware tenancy	shared	single-tenant and shared	single-tenant and shared
Internet access	automatic	automatic	no
IPv6 addressing	no	yes	yes

* Any accounts created after 12/04/2013 no longer support EC2-Classic service model.
  AWS accounts created before 03/18/2013 support both EC2-Classic and VPC services.
  Source: Amazon AWS user guide for EC2 Linux instances 2018

AWS Reserved Addressing Example

The first four IP addresses of any subnetted CIDR block are reserved for use by Amazon AWS for any VPC type. The following is an example of excluded addresses based on 10.0.0.0/16 VPC subnet addressing.

The instances assigned to the first available subnet (10.0.0.0/24) would start IP addressing for tenant instances at 10.0.0.5/24 address. The /24 subnet mask is used to subnet the 3rd octet of the CIDR block.

    10.0.0.0 = network address
    10.0.0.1 = reserved for VPC router
    10.0.0.2 = reserved for DNS services
    10.0.0.3 = reserved address
    10.0.0.255 = broadcast address

The next subnet CIDR block available is 10.0.1.0/24 with the following reserved IP addresses:

    10.0.1.0 = network address
    10.0.1.1 = reserved for VPC router
    10.0.1.2 = reserved for DNS services
    10.0.1.3 = reserved address
    10.0.1.255 = broadcast address

Subnet Models

The VPC wizard is designed to automatically deploy a VPC based on your design requirements. The following are standard pre-packaged VPC subnet models for customers.

- Public subnet only
- Public subnet and private subnet
- Public subnet and private VPN
- VPN-only subnet
- DMVPN

Public Subnet

The public subnet model is selected primarily for internet connectivity. The public subnets forward all traffic to an attached Amazon Internet gateway. The custom route table for a public subnet has a default route (0.0.0.0/0) to the Internet gateway and a local route for routing within VPC. The default route (::/0) is used for IPv6 addressing when configured. The public subnet model assigns all EC2 instances to a public subnet. In addition there are both private and public IP addresses assigned to each EC2 instance. The primary private IP address is assigned to eth0 interface. EC2 instances are assigned either a temporary IPv4 public address or a persistent (static) Elastic IP (EIP) address. The public IP address advertises IP addressing across the internet. There is a single Amazon Internet gateway required as well to enable VPC internet access.

Figure 5 Public Subnet Only

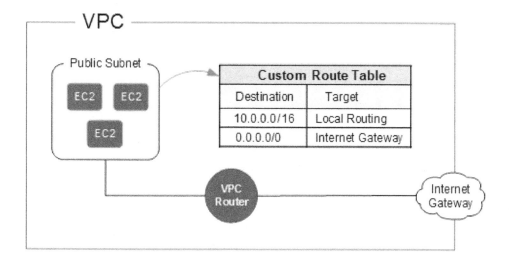

Public and Private Subnet

The public and private subnet model allows tenants to assign EC2 instances to public and private subnets. The public EC2 instances are assigned to a public subnet and private EC2 instances to a private subnet. EC2 instances in all subnets are assigned at least a single private IP address for routing within the VPC. There is a public Elastic IP (EIP) address assigned to the primary interface eth0 for instances in the public subnet as well. There is a single Amazon Internet gateway that enables public internet access. The custom route table assigned to the public subnet has a default route to the Internet gateway.

EC2 instances assigned to a private subnet are only assigned private IP addressing. There are no incoming sessions allowed from the internet to the private subnets. The tenant can assign a NAT instance to a public subnet. That will forward traffic from private subnets to the public subnet and Internet gateway for internet access. There is a default route to the NAT instance added to the main route table for the private subnet.

The private subnets can then connect to S3 storage, on-premises software and other internet-based services. Any public EC2 instance without a public EIP address can use the NAT assigned EIP for internet access as well.

Figure 6 Public and Private Subnet

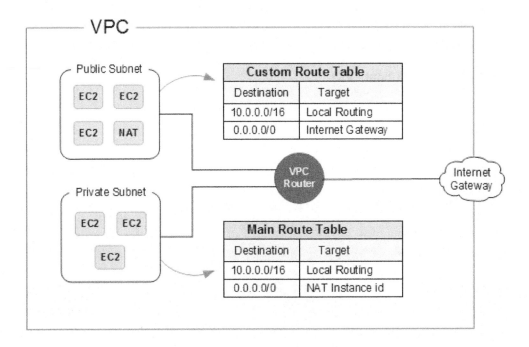

Public Subnet and Private VPN

VPN gateway enables a subnet design with public and private VPN. The public EC2 instances are assigned to a public subnet and private EC2 instances to a private VPN subnet. The tenant can deploy multiple public and private VPN subnets and route between them. The tenant attaches an Internet gateway to the VPC for public internet access. The public EC2 instances from the public subnet are assigned a private IP address and a static public EIP address. The public EIP is used to advertise EC2 instance across the internet.

Figure 7 Public Subnet and Private VPN

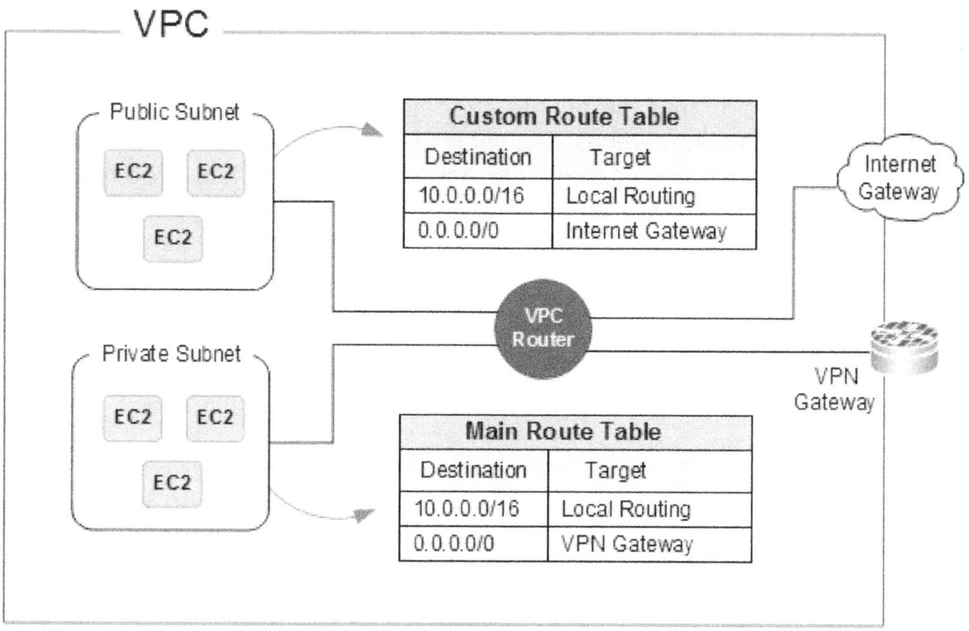

The private EC2 instances are assigned private IP addressing only. There is a single Amazon virtual private gateway (VPN) attached to the VPC. That is used for terminating VPN connections from an on-premises network. The main route table assigned to the private subnet has a default route to the VPN gateway.

Table 3 Private Subnet VPN with Internet Access

Main Route Table	
Destination	Target
10.0.0.0/16	local
172.16.0.0/24	vgw-id
0.0.0.0./0	nat-instance-id

Tenants can assign a single NAT instance in the public subnet to enable internet access for private subnet to the Internet gateway. There is a default route added to the main route table for routing to the NAT instance shown with Table 3. The private subnets can then connect to S3 storage and get company software updates for example. That is preferred to routing through the virtual private gateway and then egress across an on-premises internet connection. Any public EC2 instance without an assigned public EIP can use NAT assigned EIP for internet access as well. The main route table is updated with the subnet address used by on-premises VPN connection. You cannot assign two default routes to the same route table.

VPN-Only Subnet

VPN-only subnet model is comprised of all private subnets. There is no direct connection to the internet. EC2 instances are assigned private IP addressing only. Tenants can assign multiple private subnets to the main route table for example. The subnets communicate between them with the local route. There is a single Amazon virtual private gateway attached to the VPC. It is used for terminating VPN connection to the on-premises customer gateway. All VPC traffic with an external destination are forwarded to the virtual private gateway using the default route.

Figure 8 Private VPN-Only Subnet

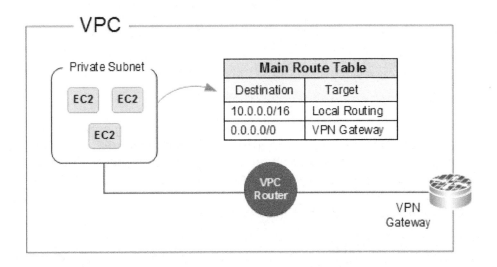

DMVPN

DMVPN is a public VPN solution based on public and private subnets. That allows the tenant to deploy a route-based VPN. In addition the DMVPN can forward traffic to internet-based services such as S3 storage. DMVPN provides dynamic routing of all protocols and on-demand VPN connectivity across the internet.

The private EC2 instances are assigned private IP addressing only. The public EC2 instances are assigned a private IP address and public EIP address. The public subnets are assigned EIP addressing for internet connectivity. The tenant attaches a virtual private gateway (VPG) or Cisco CSR 1000V to the VPC. That is used for terminating on-premises DMVPN connections. Traffic from the private and public subnets are forwarded to the VPN gateway. The tenant must attach an Internet gateway as well for internet access. Cisco CSR 1000V manages routing for internet and VPN traffic. In addition CSR 1000V supports interconnecting multiple VPCs for high availability.

Figure 9 DMVPN

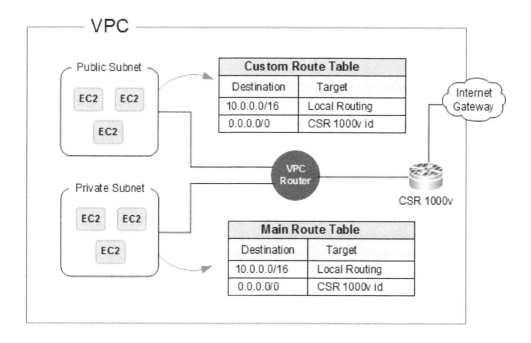

Troubleshooting Question

You are troubleshooting network connectivity to an Amazon AWS application in a private subnet and have verified access to public subnet instances. Select two components you should you verify as part of your troubleshooting process

    A. NAT instance is enabled
    B. main route table is correct
    C. custom route table is correct
    D. EIP is assigned to instances in private subnet
    E. hardware tenancy is default setting

Answer (A,B)

VPC Hardware Tenancy

VPC hardware (instance) tenancy is a global attribute that is configured when the VPC is created. The default setting is shared hardware unless configured with dedicated (single-tenant). The hardware tenancy of a VPC can be changed from dedicated to default after you create it. You cannot change the instance tenancy of a VPC to dedicated after it is created. EC2 instances are launched using the global VPC tenancy however that can be modified at launch time.

The advantages of selecting default tenancy for your VPC is compatibility with AWS services and launch support. Default tenancy permit tenants to launch an EC2 instance as either default (shared hardware) or dedicated (single-tenant) isolated hardware. Creating a VPC with dedicated tenancy only allows EC2 instances to launch as dedicated or host. The VPC does not permit running instances with default (shared) tenancy for that configuration.

There is dedicated host option as well that assigns a physical server to a tenant for running instances. It provides server-level isolation and a customizable environment. The host option is typically required for licensing or security compliance requirements. The advantages of dedicated and host tenancy is performance, reliability and security. Some AWS services do not work with a dedicated tenancy VPC and there is increased cost. The choice is based on requirements for performance and security.

    • default = instance runs on shared hardware
    • dedicated = instance runs on single-tenant isolated hardware
    • host = instance runs on isolated server that is tenant configurable

Security Groups

EC2 security group is a static virtual firewall that is associated with one or more EC2 instances within a VPC. They are provided by Amazon for EC2 instance level packet filtering. The security groups are comprised of multiple inbound and outbound permit rules assigned to an instance interface. There is a maximum of five security groups per instance and 100 security groups per VPC supported. There is no support for deny rules and reverse direction traffic is automatically permitted (stateful) for a session.

Tenants can add multiple inbound and outbound rules that permit protocols such as HTTP, ICMP and SSH. The security group is associated with a network interface assigned to an EC2 instance when it is launched. All rules are examined for a match before permitting or dropping packets.

The default security group permits all inbound and outbound traffic between all instances. . Any EC2 instance not associated with a security group during launch is associated with the default security group. EC2 instances cannot communicate when a new security group replaces the default group unless rules are added to explicitly permit it. Any new security group is unconfigured and explicitly denies all inbound and outbound traffic. The operational mode is stateful so any security group rules permitting an inbound session also permit outbound traffic for the same session by default.

AWS security group rules are comprised of source IP, protocol type and port range. You can add a description to the security group for troubleshooting.

- protocol type = TCP, UDP, ICMP, All etc.
- port number = single port or multiple (range) of application ports
- source = individual IPv4 address, IPv6 address or destination security group

All EC2 instances associated with a security group are affected by any changes to the permit rules. There are separate tables within a security group for inbound and outbound rules. There is support for single source IP address with /32 subnet mask, CIDR block range, all source IP addresses (0.0.0.0/0) and a security group id. The tenant can deploy IPv6 addressing to a VPC however AWS security groups only support prefix-length of /128 for single IPv6 address.

AWS supports Linux-based and Windows-based AMI. The security group rules assigned to EC2 instances must be updated to enable inbound SSH (Linux), RDP (Windows), and ICMP access. That permits customers to access EC2 instances from on-premises. ICMP packets are enabled for routing management traffic and Ping command.

The following example permits SSH (22) and HTTPS (443) from 200.200.1.1/32 source public address. That could be the public address of a connection from the enterprise data center. In addition HTTP and ICMP (Ping) are permitted from all source IP addresses (0.0.0.0/0).

Table 4 Security Group Inbound Rules

Protocol Type	Port Number	Source IP
TCP	22	200.200.1.1/32
TCP	443	200.200.1.1/32
TCP	80	0.0.0.0/0
ICMP	ALL	0.0.0.0/0

Troubleshooting Question

What is required to Ping from a source instance to a destination instance?

A. Network ACL: not required
   Security Group: allow ICMP outbound on source/destination EC2 instances

B. Network ACL: allow ICMP inbound/outbound on source/destination subnets
   Security Group: not required

C. Network ACL: allow ICMP inbound/outbound on source/destination subnets
   Security Group: allow ICMP outbound on source EC2 instance
   Security Group: allow ICMP inbound on destination EC2 instance

D. Network ACL: allow TCP inbound/outbound on source/destination subnets
   Security Group: allow TCP and ICMP inbound on source EC2 instance

Answer (C)

The source EC2 instance requires a security group with an outbound rule allowing ICMP. The destination EC2 instance requires a security group with an inbound rule allowing ICMP. In addition ICMP must be allowed inbound and outbound for the network ACL on each subnet where the instances are assigned. Subnets cannot span Availability Zones so there are two separate subnets and network ACLs.

- Network ACL: allow ICMP inbound and outbound on both subnets
- Security Group: allow ICMP outbound on source EC2 instance
- Security Group: allow ICMP inbound on destination EC2 instance

Network ACL

This is an optional security feature available in addition to security groups for additional packet filtering. It is the second level of defense that supports allow and deny rules for subnets. Rules are applied to packets in a numbered order for matching purposes.

Network ACL is a stateless security service that is configured and assigned to a VPC subnet. The return traffic is inspected as well so it is stateless. There are allow and deny rules supported for inbound and outbound tables per ACL. In addition you can assign the same single ACL across multiple subnets however only one ACL per subnet. Each subnet must be assigned to an ACL. The default ACL is assigned and permits all inbound and outbound IPv4 and IPv6 traffic unless a new ACL is assigned. The ACL is evaluated based on a defined order called a numbering or sequence list.

Table 5 Security Group vs Network ACL

Security Group	Network ACL
stateful	stateless
instance-level interface	subnet-level
permit rules only	permit and deny rules
all rules examined first	rules processed until match
enabled with instance launch configuration	assigned to subnet for all instances

Troubleshooting Question

You have configured a security group to allow ICMP, SSH and RDP inbound and assigned the security group to all instances in a subnet. There is no access to any Linux-based or Windows-based instances and you cannot Ping any instances. The network ACL for the subnet is configured to allow all inbound traffic to the subnet. What is the most probable cause?

A. security group and network ACL outbound rules

B. network ACL outbound rules

C. security group outbound rules

D. Bastion host required

Answer (C)

The fact that inbound rules are configured on the security group would point to the network ACL outbound rules as the problem. Security groups are stateful meaning allowing traffic inbound is all that is required. The same security group will automatically allow the same inbound traffic outbound as well.

The network ACL is stateless so that inbound rules will require matching outbound rules for a subnet where the instance resides. It isn't enough to allow inbound traffic only for the protocols. The default network ACL for each subnet allows all traffic so that customizing it would deny inbound and outbound rules unless explicitly granted.

Internet Gateway

Amazon Internet Gateways enable internet connectivity for all traffic external to the private AWS cloud. That creates a distributed network architecture with high availability. The tenant can connect with a variety of public and private services.

Internet gateway is available for connecting public subnets within a single VPC to the internet and by extension on-premises clients and applications. In addition they connect tenants to public AWS services such as S3 storage.

EC2 instances launched into a public subnet require an Internet Gateway that is automatically created with VPC wizard. In addition each EC2 instance requires a public IPv4 address to be able to communicate with the Internet. Amazon AWS provides a default of five Elastic IP addresses (EIP) to each user account.

Internet gateway provides access to the internet for all EC2 instances within a VPC. In addition it provides 1:1 Network Address Translation (NAT) from private addressing to public internet addressing for the VPC. There is horizontal scaling with virtually no bandwidth limits. The network capacity limits occur with EC2 instances or internet connection speed.

The tenant can connect with a variety of internet transport services including broadband services, MPLS and Metro Ethernet. The web servers EC2 instances are assigned to a VPC public subnet. There is only one Internet gateway assigned to each VPC. The Amazon perimeter devices inspect and forward packets to the tenant Internet gateway for any public IP (EIP) address assigned to the tenant.

Virtual Private Gateway

The purpose of virtual private gateway (VPN) is for connecting on-premises hosts and servers to a VPC. The virtual private gateway is assigned to private subnets within a VPC. That provides a secure connection for on-premises connectivity. The packets from the private subnets are forwarded to the gateway that is configured with an assigned public address. That is used for connectivity to the customer gateway.

There is only one virtual private gateway assigned to each VPC. Amazon provides a default feature that terminates VPN tunnels at redundant virtual private gateways located at different Availability Zones. That provides link redundancy and VPN gateway redundancy for the same assigned VPC.

There is support for static routing or BGP dynamic routing with assigned private ASN numbering. All data is encrypted with IPsec using AES256 cipher. Route propagation feature automatically installs local routes in the main route table for advertising to a peering customer gateway. There is a default route as well added to the main route table (0.0.0.0/0) for EC2 instances to access the virtual private gateway connection.

NAT Instance

NAT instance is assigned to the public subnet to enable packet forwarding between public and private subnets. There is a default route (0.0.0.0/0) along with *nat-instance-id* added to the main route table for routing purposes. Amazon EC2 instances perform source/destination check as a default setting. All EC2 instances must be the source or destination for any inbound or outbound packets. NAT instance is a security transit point between public and private subnets. As a result the customer must disable source/destination check for the NAT instance.

NAT Gateway vs NAT Instance

NAT gateway and NAT instance enable EC2 instances to initiate outbound packets from a private subnet to a public subnet. VPC does not allow traffic to flow directly from private to public subnets for security reasons without that. It is not the same as traditional network address translation. There is an EIP assigned to the NAT service that enables packet forwarding packets to the public subnet. The NAT gateway is a managed service that does not require the tenant to have a running EC2 instance.

Figure 10 Web-based Application Subnetting Example

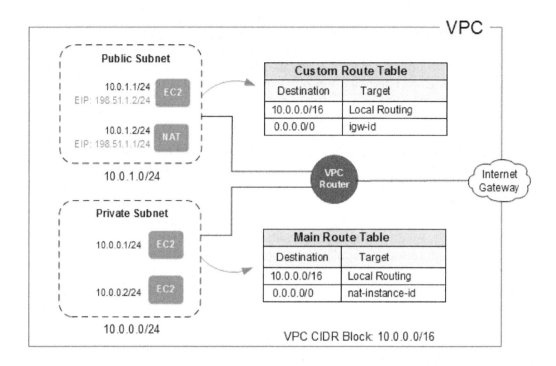

In addition NAT gateway is more scalable than NAT instance with 10 Gbps throughput for faster applications and redundant. There is no support for associating security groups with the NAT gateway.

NAT Gateway enables multiple servers on a private subnet with only a single EIP required and Availability Zone redundancy. That enable tenants to deploy a web application comprised of multiple public web servers with only private addressing assigned to instances.

NAT Gateway decreases the number of Elastic IP addresses (public) required for an application with multiple public web servers to a single EIP. In addition there is support for redundancy with multiple NAT gateways assigned to separate Availability Zones.

The tenant assigns a private (RFC 1918) IP address to each web server from the same subnet. That creates a private subnet with an associated route table that has no access to the internet. Add a NAT Gateway with an EIP to enable internet access. Add a default route to the routing table of web servers that points to the NAT Gateway.

NAT Gateway Operation

The NAT Gateway is assigned to a public subnet and as a result has a custom route table. Add a default route to the custom route table of NAT Gateway that points to the Internet Gateway. The single EIP assigned to the NAT Gateway is used to enable internet access for all web servers on a private subnet. The Elastic Load Balancer (ELB) assigned to load balance inbound traffic from the internet to all web servers is assigned to the same public subnet as the NAT Gateway and by extension same custom route table.

Outbound traffic from web server EC2 instances is first forwarded to Elastic Load Balancer (ELB) internal private address. Each instance is assigned a private IP address for internal VPC routing whether or not it has a public interface. Inbound traffic from the internet is forwarded from the Internet Gateway to NAT Gateway where it is routed within VPC to ELB.

Domain Name Services (DNS)

When an EC2 instance is launched into a default VPC, Amazon AWS provides the instance with public and/or private DNS hostnames that correspond to the public IPv4 and private IPv4 addresses for the EC2 instance. The following are DNS attributes configured when default VPC type is selected:

- DNS resolution: **yes** (enable AWS provided DNS services)
- DNS hostnames: **yes** (AWS assigns private and/or public DNS hostnames)

When an instance is launched into a nondefault VPC type, Amazon AWS provides each instance with a private DNS hostname. In addition a public DNS hostname is provided only when DNS hostnames attribute is changed from **no** to **yes** and your EC2 instance is using a public IPv4 address.

DNS attributes are changed to false (**no**) and DHCP options modified for private DNS services. That points to private DNS servers and customized DNS hostnames. The DHCP attributes "*domain-name-servers*" allow four private DNS servers to be specified. In addition the "*domain-name*" attribute is configured for the company domain name assigned.

DNS Attributes

- DNS resolution: **no** (disable AWS DNS and use tenant private DNS servers)
- DNS hostnames: **no** (tenant custom public and/or private DNS hostnames)

DHCP Options

- domain-name-servers = *your-server1…*
- domain-name = *company domain*

VPC Endpoints

VPC endpoints enable EC2 instances in private subnets to communicate directly with supported AWS services from within AWS cloud instead of traversing the internet. Currently VPC endpoints can access S3, DynamoDB and Kinesis streams services.

VPC endpoints enable tenants to create a connection from a single VPC to supported AWS services with private IP addressing only. As a result all routing is directly from a private subnet within the main route table. There is no requirement or support for the traditional solution of Internet gateway or NAT instance. Traffic is internal to the Amazon AWS cloud eliminating any support for cross-region requests.

The primary reason for deploying VPC endpoints is to minimize the costs associated with internet connectivity for S3, DynamoDB and Kinesis traffic classes. It is preferable as well to avoid performance problems inherent with internet connections. In addition all traffic remains within the AWS cloud and does not traverse the internet. That is preferred for applications with security compliance requirements.

Figure 11 VPC Endpoint for Private Connectivity to S3 Storage

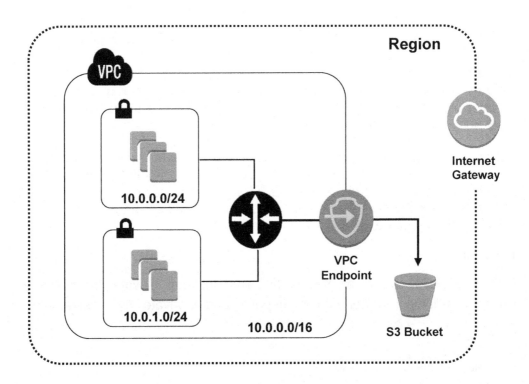

Usage costs for Internet gateway and NAT are eliminated for AWS services that support endpoints. The VPC endpoint is an Elastic Network Interface (ENI) with a private IP address assigned or AWS Private Link service. The ENI is nothing more than the EC2 instance interface that supports multiple public and/or private IP addresses. There is a Network Load Balancer that forwards requests to AWS services from a VPC endpoint for network level connectivity.

By extension any external links such as Direct connect or VPC are not supported for VPC endpoints. There is no VPC peering permitted considering traffic does not leave the source VPC. AWS permits security policies that are endpoint centric for managing access to S3 buckets as an additional layer of security where there are existing bucket permissions. VPC endpoint default policy is to allow full access to S3 buckets where there is no bucket-level or object-level permissions.

VPC Peering

VPC peering connection is a direct private connection between two VPCs that enables you to route traffic between them using private IP addresses. Instances in either VPC can communicate with each other and traffic remains within Amazon AWS cloud (not internet). The VPC peering feature can link different AWS accounts as well. There is only a single VPC peering connection permitted between two VPC's.

The required information includes neighbor VPC ID, account ID and VPC CIDR block. The VPC ID and account ID are administrative attributes that identify the AWS customer account. The tenant must add a route to the local main route table that points to the neighbor CIDR block range. The IAM cross-account access role is assigned to the initiating tenant from the neighbor that allows connection setup.

There is no support for transitive routing between VPC peering links. VPC peering is based on private point-to-point links between each VPC. The tenant cannot use a hub VPC for routing packets between two connected spoke VPCs. The spoke VPCs must be directly connected to exchange routes. That results in additional VPC links and routing between them.

Refer to the topology drawing. Your company has asked you to configure a peering link between two VPCs that are currently not connected or exchanging any packets. What destination and target is configured in the routing table of VPC1 to enable packet forwarding to VPC2?

Figure 12 VPC Peering Example

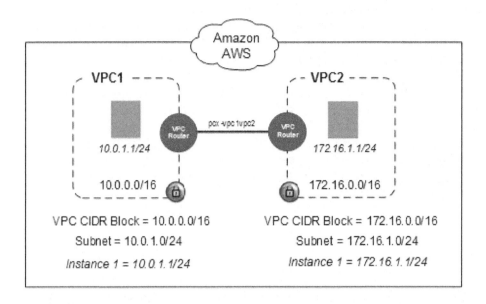

The VPC peering link (pcx-vpc1vpc2) requires a single route entry added to each VPC main route table. Any route entry is comprised of a destination and a target. The VPC1 routing table requires the following route.

destination = 172.16.0.0/16
target = pcx-vpc1vpc2

Route Table: VPC1

Destination	*Target*
10.0.0.0/16	Local
172.16.0.0/16	pcx-vpc1vpc2

Route Table: VPC2

Destination	*Target*
172.16.0.0/16	Local
10.0.0.0/16	pcx-vpc1vpc2

Overlapping IP address ranges blocks are not permitted within a VPC. The design standard is to assign 10.0.0.0/16 CIDR block for instances assigned to private subnets. The tenant can use IP addresses from any private RFC 1918 address space. The tenant would typically use /24 subnet mask to subnet the third octet. This is an example of three non-overlapping subnets (10.0.1.0/24, 10.0.2.0/24, 10.0.3.0/24) assignable to a VPC.

Transitive routing occurs when a hub VPC is used to route packets between two connected spoke VPCs. That is not supported with VPC peering. Routing only occurs between directly connected VPCs. In addition Internet Gateways and VPN Gateways are not permitted in peering VPCs. They are not required either considering all traffic is within the Amazon AWS data centers whether it is the same or inter-region traffic.

Direct Connect

Direct Connect is a private WAN service for connecting on-premises data centers directly to AWS services. The private WAN service is only available at Amazon AWS regional data centers. The advantages of Direct Connect are security, performance and reliability. The service provides high speed bandwidth for data center interconnectivity at 1 Gbps and 10 Gbps. The increased bandwidth optimizes bulk data transfers from databases and delay sensitive traffic such as voice and video.

Figure 13 Direct Connect Architecture

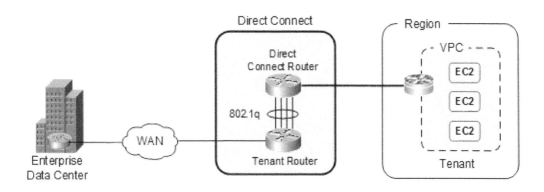

Direct Connect provides access at the AWS cloud connection point to all AWS public and private services through virtual interfaces. The public virtual interfaces are configured at the tenant colocated router for accessing S3 and Glacier storage services. In addition private virtual interfaces are configured for VPC access where application EC2 instances reside.

The purpose of BFD is to detect link failure and do fast failover to a standby link such as VPN IPsec. Direct Connect is a private and not internet-based service that is not a solution for extending on-premises VLANs to the AWS cloud. There is no active/active topology available either that negates any load balancing to the AWS cloud.

Direct Connect Advantages

The purpose of AWS Direct Connect is to enable private dedicated connection between on-premises and AWS cloud. It is often used for backups, real-time replication for hybrid cloud solutions. There is a top speed of 10 Gbps that is reliable and unaffected by any internet latency and congestions. The high performance can result in costs that are competitive or lower than internet-based services. There is no redundancy or load balancing across multiple connections however. Failover is available with a second Direct Connect service or providing VPN IPsec connection.

Table 6 Direct Connect and VPN Feature Comparison

Direct Connect	VPN
takes longer to turn up service	faster to turn-up service
higher startup and monthly cost	lower costs
higher bandwidth and scalable	lower bandwidth and less scalable
reliable private service	internet-based service is less reliable
dedicated access to AWS services	recommended for backup service

Storage Services

<u>Elastic Block Storage (EBS)</u>

Amazon Elastic Block Store is a persistent (permanent) store that is attached to an EC2 instance or database instance. It is used primarily for operating system, application and data files. It is preferred to instance store that deletes session data when the instance is terminated, stopped or problems occur. The instance store however does not delete any session data when an instance is rebooted.

Device Root Volume

The root device volume used to launch (boot) an EC2 instance is either instance store backed (S3) or an EBS-backed AMI. The EBS root volume is equivalent to a hard drive boot volume for an EC2 instance or database instance. Tenants can attach additional EBS data volumes that increase persistent storage available for an instance as well.

EBS volumes are attached to a single instance only and not shared among multiple instances. In addition multiple different EBS volumes can be attached to only one EC2 instance where one of the EBS volumes is the root device. EBS volume can only be attached and detached to an EC2 instance in the same Availability Zone. The tenant must snapshot the volume and create a new volume when migrating it to a different Availability Zone. In addition the user or AWS service must have the required IAM permissions.

Volume Type

EBS volume type is selected from General Purpose SSD (gp2), Provisioned IOPS SSD (io1), Throughput Optimized HDD (st1), Cold HDD (sc1) or Magnetic (previous generation). The instance type selected governs the performance limits of the EBS volume type selected. Each Amazon EBS volume is automatically replicated within its Availability Zone for durability.

The volume type enables disk volume size and throughput capacity. The volume type is selected based on application using the EBS volume and performance requirements. EBS is designed for a variety of application workloads such as web servers, RDS, NoSQL, EMR and data warehousing. The following are typical use cases for each EBS volume type.

✓ Provisioned IOPS SSD (io1) and large scale databases (RDS etc.)

✓ General Purpose SSD (gp2) and smaller databases

✓ Throughput Optimized HDD (magnetic st1) and big data, warehousing

✓ Cold HDD (sc1) and low cost infrequently accessed storage

Table 7 EBS Volume Type Performance Specifications

Attribute	Solid State Drive (SSD)		Hard Disk Drive (HDD)	
Volume Type	General Purpose	Provisioned IOPS	Throughput Optimized	Cold HDD
API Name	gp2	io1	st1	sc1
Volume Size	1 GB - 16 TB	4 GB - 16 TB	500 GB - 16 TB	500 GB - 16 TB
Max IOPS/Volume	10,000	32,000	500	250
Max.Throughput/Volume	160 Mbps	500 Mbps	500 Mbps	250 Mbps
Max. IOPS/Instance	80,000	80,000	80,000	80,000
Max. Throughput/Instance	1,750 Mbps	1,750 Mbps	1,750 Mbps	1,750 Mbps
Dominant Attributes	IOPS	IOPS	Mbps	Mbps

Creating EBS Volumes

Amazon EBS volume can only be attached to EC2 instance within the same Availability Zone. In addition encrypted volumes can only be attached to selected instance types. You can also create and attach EBS volumes when you launch instances by specifying a block device mapping. The following options are selectable when creating an EBS volume from EC2 console.

- Select the region to create EBS volume
- Select volume type
- Select maximum IOPS (Provisioned IOPS volume type only)
- Assign volume size (GB)
- Select availability zone
- Create an encrypted volume (Optional)
- Select master key for volume encryption (Optional)
- Add resource tags to the volume (Optional)

Amazon EBS Snapshots

EBS Snapshot is a backup of an EBS root volume and any additional EBS volumes (data) attached to an EC2 instance at a point in time. It is a bootable EBS volume that can launch EC2 instances and used to create additional AMI's when required. The recommended procedure is to stop the EC2 instance, unmount the volume and Snapshot the EBS volume for best results.

Figure 14 Copying an EBS Snapshot to a Different Availability Zone

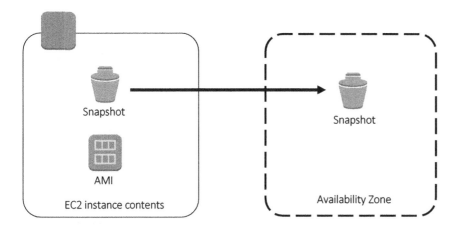

Snapshots are used to restore a point in time state including all data for a tenant. IAM users, groups and roles are assignable to EBS snapshots to specify access and administrative tasks. Encryption of data at rest is recommended based on the fact that cloud is a public shared domain.

The tenant can create a new AMI from an existing EC2 instance. Amazon EC2 creates a snapshot of your instance root volume and any other EBS volumes attached to your instance when creating a new AMI. During launch of an EC2 instance associated with the new AMI, there is a new EBS root volume created from the EBS snapshot.

There is support for copying EBS encrypted snapshots between multiple AWS accounts and cross-region. The tenant must manually configure cross-region replication from AWS services. There is a feature that copies over only snapshot changes making it faster and more cost effective. The tenant can snapshot encrypted and unencrypted EBS volumes.

Cross-Account Snapshots

It is common for tenants to create multiple AWS accounts based on function. That could include for example three accounts called development, testing and production. In addition data is moved between all three accounts based on the software lifecycle. As a result cross-account access is a key aspect of sharing data across the cloud.

The keys used to encrypt EBS snapshots (and other AWS data) is stored in and managed by AWS Key Management Service (KMS). The source account must create and share the custom key for the snapshot with the target account. In addition the encrypted EBS snapshot is shared with the target account. All of that is done from the IAM console where role or user permissions are granted.

The target account user locates the EBS encrypted volume and select a different region from the source account. It isn't uncommon for software developers to be located in different countries. There is no support for sharing EBS snapshots publicly.

EBS volumes are identified by the assigned Amazon Resource Name (ARN) and used by *CreateSnapshot* (API) to create an EBS Snapshot. There is a unique ARN assigned to each AWS resource as a unique identifier to make requests, call services or specify IAM policies.

Operational Considerations

The EBS root device volume is automatically deleted when the instance is terminated. Any additional EBS volumes that were attached at launch persist (not deleted) in addition to EBS data volumes that you attach to an existing instance. The *DeleteOnTermination* attribute can be modified to False causing the EBS root volume to persist after termination.

Customer Master Keys

AWS KMS is the key management service that generates customer master keys (CMK) used to create encrypted volumes and snapshots of encrypted volumes. There is a default CMK automatically by AWS for EBS volume encryption however tenants can create custom customer master keys. The encryption keys are then used to encrypt stored data at rest, in-transit and snapshots. You should create an EBS snapshot of the unencrypted volume for backup before starting migration.

Simple Storage Services (S3)

Multi-Purpose Data Types

Simple Storage Service is an internet-based multi-purpose storage solution used as a repository for data. It is an easier key/value object store service that supports data from multiple sources and provides multiple storage classes. In addition S3 is lower cost than EBS with similar fault tolerance and durability.

S3 is not a file-based system that can boot an operating system or run any applications. It is popular as a backup solution for cloud and on-premises data. In addition it is used extensively for hosting web applications with static content. There is encryption available for data at rest and in-transit to optimize security. The following are examples of data types stored in S3 buckets.

- Snapshots
- On-Premises backups
- CloudFront content
- Bulk data
- Multi-region store
- Database backups

Bucket

S3 bucket is a container that has one or multiple objects assigned. The tenant is assigned a key to retrieve files. There is unlimited capacity, data encryption and security rights assignable to data. Amazon assigns and stores a bucket to an availability zone. The availability zone is a data center assigned to a region.

There are multiple designated AWS regions around the world. Select the region for your availability zone/s where latency is minimized for primary and redundant connections. AWS regions are selectable based on tenant location and services availability. AWS creates and associates S3 buckets in a single region only by default. The S3 pricing model specifies that data transfer to AWS cloud is free and data transfer from cloud is billed per GB/month. The following are standard bucket limits imposed by AWS.

- 100 buckets per AWS account
- bucket ownership is not transferable
- 1000 objects per bucket

Objects

S3 objects are comprised of object data and metadata. The metadata is a set of name-value pairs that describe the object including some default metadata, such as the date last modified, and content-type and content-length. The unique identifier for each S3 object in a bucket is an assigned key.

The S3 object is addressed using a bucket name + key + optional version ID. The attributes are used to create a URL that uniquely identifies the object for access. The web services endpoint includes the region where the object is located as well a part of the URL.

Data Replication

There is synchronous replication of objects within a region. Cross-region replication is supported as well for S3 buckets to enable optimized fault tolerance. It is a bucket-level configuration on the source bucket that provides automatic asynchronous copying of objects across buckets to different AWS Regions. The source bucket and destination bucket can be owned by the same or different AWS accounts.

There is only support for cross-region replication to a single bucket. The tenant must enable versioning on each bucket for that purpose as well. In addition S3 must have permissions to replicate objects from source to destination bucket. That is enabled with security access granted through an IAM created role for S3 replication feature.

Storing data in S3 buckets across multiple Availability Zones and regions is sometime required for security compliance of an application. The support for cross-region access minimizes latency for customers and employees located in different regions. The same is true of AWS services in two different regions accessing S3 data.

Object replicas are stored using the same storage class as the source object, unless modified in the replication configuration. Note as well that replicas have the same key names and metadata. Amazon replicates each object synchronously to three Availability Zones within a region by default as well.

Storage Classes

Amazon Standard storage class provides 99.999999999% durability and availability for objects. It is designed and recommended for frequently accessed data associated with cloud application and web hosting. There is multiple replication deployed that enables high availability across multiple facilities.

Amazon Reduced Redundancy Storage (RRS) provides only 99.99% durability and availability to objects. It is recommended only for dynamic, temporary and reproducible content. Tenants often have the same content durably stored somewhere else as well. There is much less replication and can only sustain loss of data in a single facility. Amazon S3 Standard Infrequent Access as the name suggests is similar to Standard however it is recommended for less frequently accessed data such as backups.

The purpose of storage class analysis is to analyze storage access patterns and transition selected data to the best storage class. It is an S3 analytical tool that automatically identifies infrequent access patterns and transitions data to S3 Standard-Infrequent Access (IA). The tenant must configure storage class analysis policies to enable bucket monitoring. The policies also support monitoring and analysis based on S3 prefix or object tag.

Data Consistency

The PUT operation is used by a web-based application to create or update (write operations) an object to an S3 bucket. In addition S3 synchronously replicates data to multiple Availability Zones. The advantage of read-after-write consistency is no stale reads for PUT of new objects. Any user that makes a read (GET) request for the objects will have the most updated version.

It is a key aspect of any storage or database service to return updated data immediately based on a user request. S3 now provides read-after-write consistency for all AWS regions as well. There is eventual consistency for overwrite PUT and DELETE operations that sometimes returns stale data however there is somewhat lower latency and higher throughput.

Amazon S3 supports a single file object size of 5 TB however it requires Multipart Upload API feature to upload in 5 GB increments. Amazon AWS S3 is an internet-based storage service that requires an internet gateway for tenant access. The architecture defines objects of up to 5 TB in size. Objects are assigned to buckets and buckets are assigned to availability zones. In addition buckets can be assigned to multiple availability zones for failover and load balancing. Multi-AZ redundancy is enabled as a default (native) feature for S3 data storage.

Bucket Security Policies

The tenant should configure data and file security to S3 volumes based on requirements. There is encryption, replication, security controls and versioning for fault tolerance and security. AWS S3 resource-based policies include bucket policies, ACLs and query strings. Identity and Access Management allow tenants to assign S3 permissions to users, groups and roles. IAM policies are recommended where there are numerous buckets with complex permissions.

S3 bucket policies are the preferred solution for cross-account access. S3 and Glacier both support resource-based policies. Assigning object-level and bucket-level permissions in addition to IAM policies prevents users from unauthorized access and deleting files. Pre-Signed URLs for S3 objects allows upload and download of S3 objects typically for web hosting applications. That feature does not require IAM credentials.

Data Encryption Models

AWS manages server-side encryption for data at rest objects when it is enabled. The objects are encrypted and decrypted on the S3 volume. There are three options for managing customer master keys however. There is S3 managed keys (SSE-S3), customer managed keys (SSE-C) and AWS KMS managed keys (SSE-KMS). Client-side encryption for data in-transit is supported as well. It is either managed by customers or KMS service. The data is encrypted before sent to Amazon AWS cloud and decrypted before store.

Server-Side Encryption (SSE)

- Data at rest encryption (AES 256)
- SSE-S3 (customer master key is S3-managed)
- SSE-C (customer master key is customer-managed)
- SSE-KMS (customer master key is AWS-managed)

Client-Side Encryption (CSE)

- Data in-transit encryption
- Customer-side managed master key
- KMS-managed customer master key

There are a variety of additional features that protect data at rest on S3 volumes. Versioning (disable by default) creates a new version of any file that is deleted or modified. That allows tenants to restore a file that was accidentally deleted. S3 versioning permits multiple versions of an object.

S3 vs Elastic Block Storage

EBS is similar to a traditional hard drive that uses block level storage and requires formatting a file system. It is directly assigned to a single EC2 instance for persistent storage and fast. EBS volume snapshots are easy to create and store on S3 buckets. In addition you can create AMI from an EBS snapshot. That allows you to modify and save a new AMI for some different usage. S3 is an internet-based multi-purpose storage solution used as a repository for data.

Table 8 Feature Comparison of S3 and Elastic Block Storage

S3	EBS
Multiple AWS services	EC2 instances, database instances
Read and write store	Mountable boot volume
Virtually unlimited store	Lower storage limits
Multiple instances	Single instance
Write update delays	No consistency model (immediate)
IAM, bucket policies	Security group, IAM
Data persistent after instance terminated	Data deleted after instance terminated
100 PUT/LIST/DELETE requests per second scalable to 300	4000 IOPS/sec

S3 Storage Use Cases

❖ You have an application that collects monitoring data from 10,000 sensors (IoT) deployed in the USA. The datapoints are comprised of video events for home security and environment status alerts. The IoT sensors only perform write operations and send event-triggered data. The application will be deployed to AWS with EC2 instances as data collectors. S3 is preferred for storing video files from sensors. Video events delivered from IoT sensors require larger file size storage. It is event-based and write operation performed only when a security alert occurs. Amazon S3 is well suited for storing fewer larger files (videos) as objects when deploying an IOT solution. In addition there is lifecycle management where data can be migrated to Glacier vaults.

❖ Your company is publishing an online catalog of books that is currently using DynamoDB for storing the information associated with each item. There is a requirement to add images for each book. DynamoDB is a one-dimensional data structure that stores a large amount of information. It is based on store and lookup and doesn't support the complex queries associated with relational databases (RDS etc). It is often used for store and search of log files as well. There is however an item limit of 400 KB that is often less than what is required for images. S3 is designed to store objects up to 5 GB per PUT and 5 TB maximum size that is cost effective and with low latency.

S3 Limitations

S3 does have an object file size limit of 5 TB however there is no limit on the number of objects (virtually unlimited). There is no support for provisioned IOPS (databases only) or support for dynamic web content. Tenants can only deploy static web content to S3 storage. The bucket names are globally unique and lowercase with a default of only 100 per account. Amazon S3 provides the Multi-Object Delete API that you can use to delete up to 1000 objects in a single HTTP request. AWS recommends deployment of best practices if the number of PUT/LIST/DELETE requests per second exceeds 100 or 300 GET requests

Glacier

Amazon Glacier is a cost effective cloud storage solution used mostly for archiving data. The tenant can use it to backup data from S3 buckets as well for additional data redundancy or for data that is not accessed that frequently.

Most AWS services require tenants to select some encryption technique when it is available. It is typically a choice of client-side or server-side encryption that determines key management and tenant responsibility. In addition there is support for in-transit and data at rest encryption for data security. AWS Glacier provides native encryption of tenant data.

Archives

Glacier stores data as files called archives. AWS assigns a unique ID to each archive for naming purposes. There is support for a single file or aggregating multiple files to a single TAR or ZIP file. The total volume of data and number of archives you can store are unlimited. Amazon AWS charges less when files are aggregated and maximum file size is 40 TB archive. Multipart upload API enables uploading an archive in parts. It is recommended when archives are larger than 100 MB.

Vaults

Vault is a container that allows storage of an unlimited number of archives. Amazon supports grouping of archives and adding vault-level security policies through Identity and Access Management (IAM). There is a notification service as well per vault that alerts tenants when files are ready for download. AWS vaults are accessed with a unique URL based on region, vault name and account ID. There is a limit of 1000 vaults permitted per AWS account in any single region.

Retrieval Options

Glacier is a popular solution for storage of S3 objects. The tenant must restore a temporary copy of any object/s first to an S3 bucket when doing a restore operation from Glacier. In addition Amazon AWS only permits initiating restore operations from the AWS S3 console. AWS offers expedited, standard and bulk service levels for retrieving data. The cost to tenants is what differentiates the service level provided.

The most reliable service is expedited that includes provisioned and on-demand options. There is a fixed monthly cost for provisioned capacity that is most reliable and recommended when tenants are retrieving high volumes of data. Tenant data is restored within an average of 1-5 minutes.

In addition there is on-demand service level that is similar to EC2 on-demand instance service and available most of the time. Standard retrieval is a lower cost service and the default when no retrieval service is explicitly configured. The average restore time however is 3-5 hours. Bulk retrieval is the least cost option however retrieval times are typically 5-12 hours.

Job Request

Job requests are created to retrieve archives and vault inventory lists. The job is queued and download is an asynchronous operation. Tenants can configure an SNS topic where Glacier can post notification after the job is completed. In addition specify an SNS topic per job request. The notification is sent only after Glacier completes the job. Configure vault notifications for a vault as well so that job notifications are sent for all retrievals.

Table 9 Feature Comparison for S3 and Glacier Storage

S3	Glacier
Frequently accessed data	Infrequently accessed data
Buckets and objects	Vaults and archives
Lower latency	Higher latency
Higher cost	Lower cost
EC2 instance store	Redundant solution for S3 data
Fast GET operation to access object	Job request to retrieve archive

AWS Storage Gateway

Amazon AWS Storage Gateway is a hybrid solution that supports storing some or all data on-premises for faster performance. The Gateway is a software (virtual) appliance that is deployed on-premises. AWS Storage Gateway provides native encryption of tenant data. The following is a list of AWS storage gateway options that store some or all data in the cloud.

- Stored Volume Gateway
- Cached Volume Gateway
- Tape Gateway (VTL)

Stored Volume Gateway

The stored volume gateway is used to store your primary data locally and asynchronously backing up that data to an S3 volume or Elastic Block Store (EBS) snapshots. Stored volumes provide low latency and security for all data considering it is stored on-premises. In addition there are data backups to AWS store for durability and fault tolerance. There is increased hardware costs for deploying additional storage capacity at the on-premises storage gateway.

You can create storage volumes and mount them as iSCSI devices from your on-premises application servers. All application data is immediately written to your local stored volumes. There is support for stored volumes that range from 1 GB to 16 TB. Each gateway configured for stored volumes can support up to 32 volumes and a total volume storage of 512 TB (0.5 PB). Data written to your stored volumes is stored on your on-premises storage hardware. AWS storage gateway stores incoming data to an upload buffer where it is asynchronously backed up to an S3 volume or an EBS snapshots.

The data is sent over an encrypted SSL connection to the AWS Storage Gateway service running in the AWS Cloud. The service then stores the data encrypted in Amazon S3 or EBS.

Cached Volume Gateway

The purpose of volume gateways is to minimize latency and enable a durable backup solution for on-premises application data. The difference between cached volumes and stored volumes is where the data is stored. The cached volume gateway stores all data within the AWS cloud on S3 buckets. Any frequently accessed data is cached on-premises to AWS storage gateway.

It is a lower cost solution that requires less capacity and scalability for the on-premises storage gateway. There is however some additional latency when requesting data that is not cached locally.

The request must be forwarded to S3 storage volume in the cloud. There is support for storage volumes up to 32 TB in size and attach to them as iSCSI devices from your on-premises application servers. Cached volumes can be created from 1 GB to 32 TB in size (rounded to nearest GB). Each gateway enabled for cached volumes can support up to 32 volumes for a total maximum storage volume of 1,024 TB (1 PB).

The on-premises application first stores any new data to the on-premises storage gateway used for cache storage. The data is then uploaded to an Amazon S3 storage volume from the upload buffer with an SSL encrypted connection. The gateway will first check the local cache storage when requesting some data before requesting it from Amazon S3. All data is encrypted at rest using server-side encryption (SSE) on S3 volumes. Amazon recommends allocating at least 20 percent of your existing file store size as cache storage. Cache storage should also be larger than the upload buffer.

Tape Gateway (VTL)

Tape Gateway is an archive solution for storing large amounts of on-premises data in the AWS Cloud. It is based on a virtual tape library (VTL) interface that enables tenants to use existing tape-based backup infrastructure. The data is stored on virtual tape cartridges that you create on your tape gateway. Each tape gateway is preconfigured with a media changer and tape drives accessed as iSCSI devices. The tape cartridges are added based on capacity requirements to archive data.

Snowball

The recommended solution for moving the most amount of on-premises data to AWS cloud as fast as possible is AWS Snowball. It is an appliance-based storage device shipped to the tenant where up to 50 TB of data can be loaded. The appliance is shipped back to the tenant where AWS receives it and copies data over to AWS S3 storage.

There is support for multiple appliances with concurrent data transfers and 256-bit encryption of data at rest. Snowball is recommended as a replacement for AWS Import/Export particularly with data transfers larger than 10 TB to S3 buckets. Snowball jobs are created from AWS management console and a Snowball appliance is automatically shipped on-premises.

AWS Import/Export

The primary on-premises solutions for data backups to S3 buckets are AWS Import/Export, Snowball and Storage Gateway. The cost, speed and recovery time is what differentiates the services. The other options are not part of any on-premises backup solution to AWS. Direct Connect is a high speed private cloud link that is available as well for copying large amounts of data.

Amazon Import/Export supports transferring on-premises data to portable storage devices. The portable devices are then shipped to Amazon support engineers where data is copied to S3 buckets and/or Glacier vaults. It is recommended when migrating less than 16 TB of on-premises data to S3 or EBS storage volumes. It is more cost effective and faster than traditional data transfer methods across the internet for bulk data.

Elastic File System (EFS)

Elastic File System enables what is essentially a file server in the cloud. The EFS is associated with a single VPC where users with security permissions can access and share files. The Elastic File System is a managed service that is created and mounted on single or multiple Linux-based EC2 instances to enable data file storage and sharing. EFS provides file locking and strong consistency that is characteristic of a file system. In addition there is support for mounting EFS file systems within your VPC to any on-premises servers for migrate, backup or workload purposes. It allows thousands of EC2 instances to simultaneously upload, access, delete and share files.

EFS expands and shrinks based on when files are added or deleted. EBS storage is basically a hard drive volume attached to a single EC2 instance. It is used directly by servers for instance to run system files and store some application data. S3 is a publicly accessible service that stores objects of all sizes including logs for backup purposes.

Mount Target

The mount target is a network interface used for communicating between multiple EC2 instances within an Availability Zone and EFS. The tenant would create a mount target in each Availability Zone for a region where tenants require access. The mount target can only be configured within a single VPC at a time. The mount targets must be deleted from the current VPC and then create new mount targets in a different VPC. That allows access to file system from EC2 instances assigned to that VPC. The mount target IP address is assigned to the same subnet as the Availability Zone where EC2 instances reside. Where there are multiple subnets for EC2 instances, pick any one subnet for that Availability Zone.

Figure 15 Elastic File System (EFS)

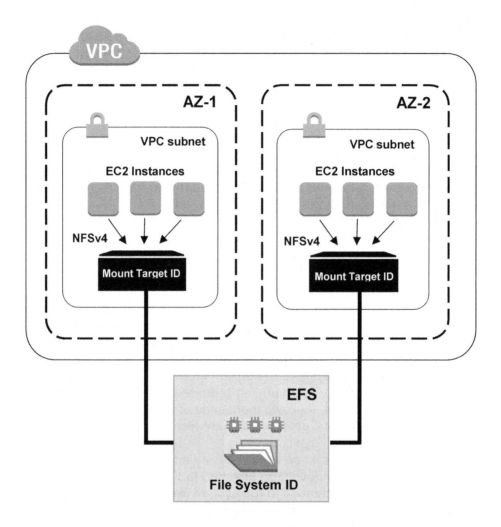

The DNS name resolves the IP address when connecting to the EFS. You can access EFS from any Linux or Windows client that supports NFSv4. The current EFS architecture only supports Linux-based EC2 instances. The protocol used for communicating between EC2 and EFS is NFSv4. There is no support currently for cross-region access of an EFS.

Allowing access between EC2 instance and mount target instance requires the tenant to modify the security groups assigned to each so the traffic flow is permitted. The source is the security group ID of the EC2 instance. The tenant must add the following rule to the security group that is assigned to the mount target instance.

Type = NFS, protocol = TCP, port = 2049, source = sg-3456scde

Migrating Files to EFS

The fastest method for copying on-premises files to EFS is with Direct Connect and File Sync. Amazon AWS recommends Direct Connect for high throughput low latency connections between on-premises and AWS cloud services. It is a private connection that when used in concert with File Sync provides best performance when copying large files frequently. It is the most costly option available as well.

Direct Connect allows tenants to mount an EFS file system from on-premises where files can be moved between servers for various applications. It is commonly referred to as a hybrid cloud where at least one server for an application resides on-premises. The advantage of File Sync is that is can copy on-premises files across any network connection to AWS cloud. It is 5 times faster than standard Linux tools and data is encrypted in transit with integrity checks on the link.

Security Architecture

AWS Account Credentials

When you first create an Amazon Web Services (AWS) account, you begin with a single sign-in identity that has complete access to all AWS services and resources in the account. This identity is called the AWS account root user and is accessed by signing in with the email address and password that you used to create the account.

Amazon AWS require tenants to provide identity credentials for sign-on to the cloud. The AWS management console requires your password. In addition there is an option to create access keys that are associated with your AWS account. They are used for access to the command line interface (CLI) or making API programmatic calls. The user or application identity is verified with access keys when making API programmatic calls.

Amazon AWS however does not recommend tenants use the AWS account credentials for access to the cloud. It is a root level access that permit unlimited access to any user that has the credentials. Root level access should only be used for administrative tasks such as billing and modifying account services.

Identity and Access Management (IAM)

Identity and Access Management (IAM) is the security schema that defines access to AWS resources for each tenant and associated AWS account/s. Each tenant has multiple users that require various security access to AWS services. The IAM defines users, groups and roles to create granular security permissions based on security access requirements. IAM security is globally unified across AWS for tenant accounts. The tenant does not have to create new roles for instance in different regions or Availability Zones. It is unified globally where existing groups and roles are centrally assigned, modified or added.

Identity-Based vs Resource-Based Permissions

IAM security model defines identity-based policies that are attached to a user, group or role. The policies are assign permissions to user, group or role for AWS services. For example EC2, RDS and DynamoDB use identity-based policies. That is in contrast to resource-based policies that are attached to resources such as S3 buckets, SQS queues and KMS encryption keys. They are permissions such as read/write access for example granted to user account ID of the requestor. It is the S3 bucket policy that verifies access when requested. Amazon S3 and Glacier storage support policies for IAM users and resource-based bucket policies.

IAM User

The tenant starts with creating multiple IAM users within an AWS account that represents employees in an organization. Each user generates a password for access to the AWS Management Console. There is an option to create an access key for each user that enable programmatic API calls to AWS resources. Typically users in an AWS account have multiple policies that represent all permissions for that user. Amazon AWS security schema is based on least privilege where any actions or resources not explicitly allowed are summarily denied by default.

The policy summary table includes a list of services and within each service there is a service table with a list of actions and associated permissions assigned. In addition there is an action table that defines resources and conditions for the specified action.

IAM Group

IAM groups are defined as a collection of IAM users. The purpose of groups is to specify permissions that can be assigned to multiple users. The advantage is easier administration of security permissions particularly when there are a lot of users to manage. It is easier to create a group and grant permissions to that single group. The permissions could represent a particular job responsibility or requirement for access to an application. The users are then assigned to that group. You can remove users or add new users based on requirements and organizational changes much easier.

- Users can be assigned to multiple groups.
- Assigning groups to other groups (nesting) is not supported.
- AWS limits number of groups and how many users can be a member

Role-Based Permissions

The IAM role grants temporary permission to a user or application for some specific purpose. Any permission the role grants do not add to the permissions already granted to the user or application. When there is a role switch any previous permissions are dropped in exchange for permissions granted with the new role. The previous (original) permissions are automatically restored when the role is removed from user or application.

There is support for attaching an IAM role to an existing EC2 instance from the EC2 console. You can also use the EC2 console to replace an IAM role attached to an existing instance. You can attach an identity-based permissions policy to an IAM role to grant cross-account permissions. The purpose of an IAM role is to grant permission to a user, AWS service or application. The role is a defined set of policies that permit access to an AWS resource.

For example a database administrator could grant cross-account permissions to a developer in account APPDEV. The access would allow the developer to copy data to an S3 bucket owned by the database administrator. The following are steps required for granting cross-account permission to an S3 bucket.

1. The database administrator creates an IAM role and assigns APPDEV account to it.

2. The database administrator attaches a permissions policy to the role that grants permissions for account APPDEV to access S3 bucket.

3. The database administrator attaches a trust policy to the role identifying account APPDEV as the principal who can assume the role.

Identity and Access Management (IAM) role is created by the administrator and assigned read-only permission to access an S3 bucket. The EC2 instance (application) is launched with the role and accesses the file on an S3 bucket.

Resource-Based Policies vs IAM Role

The trusted account permissions granted to the tenant are not replaced when resource-based security policies are deployed. The resource that you want to share must support resource-based policies. The resource-based policy is comprised of AWS account ID numbers that can access a resource. Role permissions replace any tenant account permission they were granted with the trusted account with the trusting account. Tenant retains all security permissions from trusted and trusting account that were granted when resource-based policies are used.

Amazon AWS Key Pair

Amazon AWS EC2 Linux instances do not have passwords. Instead a key pair is created for launching and login to EC2 instances within a region. The tenant connects to an EC2 instance from an SSH client. The key pair name is provided when launching an EC2 instance and tenant authenticates with the private key name to logon. The tenant must create a key pair in each region when launching instances in multiple regions

Step 1: Sign in to AWS using the URL created

Step 2: Open Amazon EC2 console from the AWS dashboard.

Step 3: Select a region for the key pair from the navigation bar.

Step 4: Select **Network** and **Security** from navigation pane, select **Key Pairs**.

Step 5: Select **Create Key Pair**, enter a name for new key pair and then **Create**.

AWS recommends assigning a name for your key that is easy to remember For example your IAM user name along with -key-pair and region name where key was created (**cisconet-key-pair-useast2**).

The private key file is automatically downloaded by your browser. The base file name is the name you specified as the name of your key pair, and the file name extension is **.pem**. Save the private key file in a safe place. The key pair name of your key pair is required by AWS when launching an instance in a region and the associated private key each time you connect to an EC2 instance.

RSA asymmetric keys include a public key and a private key. The tenant must download and store the private key themselves. In addition there is access to the EC2 instance with SSH (Linux) or Windows (RDP) and authentication at the operating system level.

Key Management Service (KMS)

Key Management Service (KMS) is a managed service that allows tenants to create and manage encryption keys. It uses Hardware Security Modules (HSMs) to protect tenant keys. AWS KMS is integrated with multiple AWS services and provides native integration with S3 and EBS. Tenants can import and rotate keys, define user policies and audit activity from the AWS Management Console or by using the AWS SDK or CLI. There is centralized access control and audit of master keys for encrypting and decrypting user data.

KMS service allows you to create, rotate, delete, disable and audit Customer Master Key (CMK) encryption keys from the IAM console. It provides centralized control over encryption and decryption of data based on defined IAM policies for users, roles and cross-account access to use a CMK. There is integration with CloudTrail as well to audit all CMK usage transactions for security compliance requirements.

AWS offers various options to manage and import keys from a customer KMI (key management infrastructure) to KMS. There are customer-managed, AWS managed and hybrid management of keys. The primary difference between the models for customer-managed encryption keys is where keys are stored.

Shared Responsibility Model

Amazon AWS tenants are responsible for monitoring of guest operating system and application level security. That includes security updates, maintenance, fixes and appliances that protect tenant data. In addition there are compliance issues and user authentication that tenants must deploy. Monitoring of application level and operating system metrics is the responsibility of tenants.

Security Best Practices

Root User

Amazon AWS recommends that you do not use your root user credentials to access AWS cloud services. In addition delete the root user access keys and use it only for intended purposes. That would include modifying support plans, billing and activating various services. The root user has unlimited access to all AWS cloud services associated with an account. It is not possible to assign security permissions that limit root user access.

Administrator Group

Create a user within Identity and Access Management (IAM) and create an administrator group. In addition, attach the AWS *AdministratorAccess* managed policy and assign them to the group. That enables them to create multiple IAM users and define individual security access for a variety of cloud services.
You can then access AWS using a special URL and the credentials for the IAM user. The alternative is to grant an IAM user administrative permissions directly.

Multiple IAM Users

Create a single AWS account with multiple IAM users that explicitly grant security permissions for various security levels and requirements. In addition create multiple AWS accounts each with IAM users per account for a granular permissions schema. IAM supports assigning security policies to a group and adding multiple users to the IAM group. That makes it easier to grant access for a single AWS account.

Grant Least Privilege

AWS has a best practice called - *Grant Least Privilege*, that recommends initially assigning the minimum security permissions to an IAM user that permits doing the requested work. Increase security access for the user based on requirements and functionality. The user access levels include List, Read, Write and Permissions. Granting the permissions access level allows the user to perform security administrator tasks for the cloud service. That could include changing security permission for access to an S3 bucket.

Multi-Factor Authentication

Amazon AWS provides a service called Multi-factor authentication (MFA) that is similar to the well-known Two-Factor Authentication. The tenant is prompted for an authentication code after providing the required username and password. It adds additional credentials to verify users before access to data is granted.

The best strategy is to explicitly assign permissions to an IAM group that allow or prevent specific activities. That would include read-only access to prevent deletion or overwrite. They are common problems in addition to file read access for privacy or granting a user administrative privileges. AWS identity credentials only apply to AWS managed infrastructure (S3 buckets etc.) however they often work in concert with tenant application credentials.

Security Token Service (STS)

AWS Security Token Service (AWS STS) enables trusted users with temporary security credentials to access AWS services. That could include existing IAM users that have permanent security credentials or temporary users that do not. The intent is to allow access for up to hour by default and then revoke access.

Any new access required would require a new STS request for the user. The advantage is the security access is not stored, does not become part of any application configuration or AWS security schema. The user can request new credentials, as long as the user requesting them still has permissions to do so at or before the expiry time. The US east-region is default for requesting STS services however multiple regions are supported.

IAM registered users have existing security permission based on granted access to AWS. User with an existing IAM identity and associated security credentials are granted temporary access through IAM. The temporary user with no existing IAM identity account are authenticated from an external on-premises federated store with SAML for Single Sign-on. The user makes a request for AWS access that is forwarded to an on-premises identity provider (IdP).

Identity Provider (IdP)

IdP then authenticates user credentials to an identity store (LDAP, ADS etc) and generates a SAML security token. The security token is forwarded to AWS STS via *AssumeRoleWithSAML* API call. The API returns credentials for the temporary session to the user. They consist of an access key ID, secret access key and security session token. The permissions to access AWS services are granted as a a result through private Federated identity.

Figure 16 AWS Security Token Service with SAML Federation

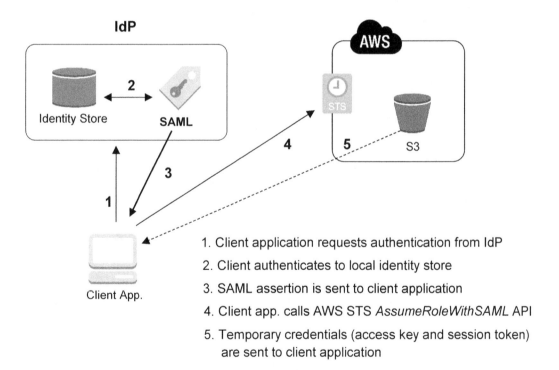

1. Client application requests authentication from IdP
2. Client authenticates to local identity store
3. SAML assertion is sent to client application
4. Client app. calls AWS STS *AssumeRoleWithSAML* API
5. Temporary credentials (access key and session token) are sent to client application

Web Identity Federation

There is Web Identity Federation as well where credentials from well-known supported platforms such as Facebook and Google are used to access AWS services. Web Federated Identity does not require distribution of access keys either for added security.

AWS supports multiple OpenID Connect (OIDC) providers with well-known identity providers (Facebook, Google etc) for web identity federation. That enables mobile web-based applications to sign-in without creating a custom sign-in for customers.

Bastion Host

The purpose of a Bastion host is to provide a security zone between a public subnet and private subnet to minimize the attack surface. It is a proxy that prevents direct access for SSH/RDP connections from the internet to private subnet EC2 instances. As a result tenants can access and manage EC2 instances through the Bastion host. The following lists the requirements for deploying a Bastion host for SSH only.

- Bastion host deployed to each public subnet
- Security group assigned to Bastion host instance with SSH allowed inbound
- Network ACL with SSH allowed inbound and outbound
- NAT instance to forward packets from public subnet to private subnet

DDoS Mitigation

The most common strategies for mitigating Distributed Denial of Service (DDoS) attacks include horizontal scaling, WAF, Bastion host, security groups, ACL, CloudWatch and minimizing attack surface.

- Horizontal scaling is enabled with Elastic Load Balancer and Auto-Scaling architecture to add capacity allowing time to detect and mitigate.

- Web Application Firewall is integrated with CloudFront and can detect DDoS request traffic patterns with web ACLs and mitigate attacks. It provides packet inspection and malware filtering in front of web servers.

- Bastion host whitelist of IP addresses denies traffic from any sources that are not approved.

- AWS provide static filtering methods available to tenants for inbound and outbound traffic. That includes security groups and Network ACLs assignable to each VPC.

- CloudWatch can be configured to alert when unusual traffic loads are occurring to respond accordingly and mitigate effects of any attack.

Web Application Firewall

The purpose of a Web Application Firewall (WAF) is to protect web-based applications from common internet web exploits. AWS WAF enables custom filtering rules that allow tenants control over what traffic is permitted or denied. For example create custom rules that block common attacks such as SQL injection or cross-site scripting. There is API support as well for automating web security rules. It is pay as you go where pricing is based on the number of rules deployed and web requests to a web application.

Security Zones

Migrating applications to the cloud require the same complex granular security policies defined at the enterprise data center. The Cisco Virtual Security Gateway (VSG) is a Layer 2 distributed firewall for east-west traffic between EC2 instances. It is a standalone appliance deployed as an EC2 instance.

The VSG works in concert with the Cisco Nexus 1000V switch to enforce logical security zones. There are security policies that must be configured between public and private server zones. There are AWS security groups available as well that support inbound and outbound rules for traffic between EC2 instances.

SAML Authentication

Tenants must configure a SAML identity provider (IdP) that sends claims required by AWS security schema. In addition IAM is used to create a SAML provider entity in your AWS account that represents your identity provider and create an IAM role that specifies you as a SAML provider in its trust policy.

Security Assertion Markup Language (SAML) is used to authorize access to SAML-enabled SaaS applications after network authentication is approved. The SaaS applications have additional security that authorize specific features and data access. The tenant can use LDAP or SAML for directory services and application security. SAML is more suited to cloud applications with additional features that improve security and ease management.

SAML enables federated Single Sign-On (SSO) to integrate authentication and authorization for end users. Single Sign-On authorizes a user to all applications instead of having to sign-on to multiple servers and services. SAML has many advantages compared with LDAP for cloud-based SaaS applications. The SaaS management portal allow tenants to configure stringent password policies. That optimizes security for application and database security compliance.

Amazon Inspector

Amazon Inspector is an automated security assessment service that analyzes the posture of your AWS deployment. Amazon Inspector provides vulnerability assessment testing on tenant applications to verify what if any known vulnerabilities exist. In addition there is analysis of compliance with best practices. The results are listed in a report sent to the tenant that is prioritized by level of severity. Amazon Inspector is comprised of a knowledge base with hundreds of rules for security best practices and vulnerability definitions.

Amazon Inspector is a security assessment service from AWS that scans tenant infrastructure for security vulnerabilities and makes recommendations. That is based on known current vulnerabilities with applications for example. Trusted Advisor is used for cost optimization in addition to advising tenants on best practices for performance optimization and security.

AD Connector vs Simple AD

Simple AD

- standalone directory in the cloud
- ADS managed service with limited scalability
- support for compatible AWS applications
- support Linux workloads that need LDAP service
- AWS automatically create daily snapshot of the directory
- Windows EC2 instances join to the Simple AD

AD Connector

- provides increased scalability
- authentication request sent to on-premises ADS (proxy)
- integration and login to compatible AWS applications
- IAM role integration and single sign-on for console users
- support for multi-factor authentication (MFA)
- VPN or Direct Connect service required

Database Services

The database instance includes all compute and storage attributes assigned to a database/s. It defines all components and settings of a full-fledged database environment. Amazon AWS tenants often have multiple database instances for high availability and failover purposes assigned to a private subnet. The tenant must assign a security group to a database instance. In addition DNS hostname and DNS resolution attributes are configured to resolve DNS requests.

DynamoDB

Standard Features

DynamoDB is a NoSQL managed database service that is deployed for applications that require fast concurrent read/write lookups for smaller records with low latency (msec). In addition DynamoDB is well suited to store and retrieval of frequently accessed records. It supports multiple store models such as documents and key-value. There is virtually unlimited scalability that is added automatically based on throughput and storage requirements.

DynamoDB allocates storage for tables in partitions using solid-state drives (SSDs) and automatically replicated across three Availability Zones within an AWS Region. The automatic partitioning model seamlessly distributes the data across multiple partitions for scaling of storage capacity.

The maximum size of an item (record) that can be stored in a DynamoDB table is 400 KB. Tenants can store large attributes as an S3 object for items that exceed the maximum 400 KB limit. There is support for a variety of data types including JSON documents, web session state and blobs.

There is only client-side encryption (Java) available to tenants that are using DynamoDB database services. The tenant obtains an encryption key from AWS KMS service for that purpose. All data is encrypted while it is in-transit and at rest on DynamoDB. AWS KMS is used to decrypt keys when requests are made from tenant.

Data Replication and Consistency

DynamoDB provides tenants with different storage classes. There is write replication of data across tables in three Availability Zones within the same region. That enables durability and fault tolerance for tenant applications. DynamoDB returns **HTTP 200** code to your application when all copies of the data are updated to all zones.

The default consistency model used by DynamoDB is eventually consistent. It provides higher throughput and lower latency however stale reads (not current) are sometimes returned. Tenants can select strongly consistent model that provides the most updated data that is not stale. The data is eventually consistent across all storage locations typically within one second or less.

Figure 17 IoT Sensor Processing with Analytic and Store Services

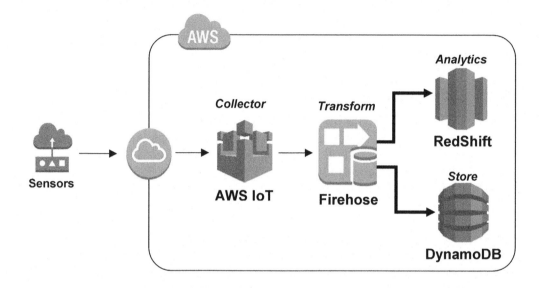

Read/Write Capacity Calculation

You must specify strongly consistent read and write capacity for your DynamoDB database. You have determined read capacity of 128 Kbps and write capacity of 25 Kbps is required for your application. What is the read and write capacity units required for DynamoDB table?

A. 32 read units, 25 write units

B. 1 read unit, 1 write unit

C. 16 read units, 2.5 write units

D. 64 read units, 10 write units

Answer (A)

DynamoDB specifies one read capacity unit as a single read per second for an item (record) up to 4 KB in size. In addition one write capacity unit as a single write per second for an item of up to 1 KB in size. The read capacity of 128 Kbps would require 32 read units (128 kbps = 4 KB x 32 units). The write capacity of 25 Kbps would require 25 write units (25 Kbps = 1 KB x 25 units).

Capacity Management

DynamoDB supports a feature called Auto Scaling that allows tenants to configure a range of capacity units with a maximum value. That enables capacity units to be increased temporarily during periods of peak traffic and prevent throttling.

DynamoDB publishes capacity metrics to CloudWatch and any exceeded event triggers a CloudWatch alarm and SNS notification. The alarm then invokes the Auto Scaling feature within DynamoDB to increase or decrease capacity units.

DynamoDB will automatically throttle read or write requests when they exceed current throughput configured settings. That includes requests to a table or an index. The purpose of throttling is to prevent an application from consuming too many capacity units. Amazon AWS returns **HTTP 400** code (Bad Request) when throttling is initiated.

DynamoDB Use Cases

Typical use cases include storing metadata for S3 objects that enable complex index and searches. In addition with the streams feature enabled there is store and retrieve for web page clickstreams and IoT sensor data. DynamoDB is used a lot for dynamic data that often requires increased storage over time.

❖ You have a requirement to create an index to search customer objects stored in S3 buckets. The solution should enable you to create a metadata search index for each object stored to an S3 bucket. The easiest most scalable solution is to use DynamoDB (or Elasticsearch) for storing metadata index. Front end EC2 instances are used as data collectors that forward objects to S3 buckets. Create a Lambda function that is invoked by an S3 bucket event notification when a new object is created. The Lambda function updates DynamoDB table with an index entry for the new object.

❖ DynamoDB is a preferred solution for IoT sensor data there are frequent (thousands) of datapoint read/writes per minute. IoT sensors can write directly to DynamoDB tables. The datapoint range support is from 1 byte to 400 KB. In addition it is designed for frequent access and fast lookup of smaller records. S3 is less structured and creates a single file for each event this is cumbersome. In addition Firehose is typically required for datapoint write operations to S3. Moving sensor data from DynamoDB to RedShift for analytics is easier as well. Consider for example creating time series tables for sensor data based on time stamps.

Relational Database Service (RDS)

Managed Services

Amazon RDS is a managed relational database service. There is support for multiple database engines including Aurora, PostgreSQL, MySQL, MariaDB, Oracle and Microsoft SQL Server. It is often used to migrate on-premises applications such as Oracle to the cloud for administrative offload. The metrics used for RDS billing include instance class, hourly access and storage usage (GB/month).

It is designed to provide database ready services to tenants with minimal setup. The tenant is responsible for any application level configuration, security groups and IAM policies. VPC security groups enable EC2 instances and RDS instance to share the same security group within a VPC. The purpose is to control access to database instances and EC2 instances inside a VPC. EC2 security groups by contrast control access to an EC2 instance only.

Amazon installs instances, assigns capacity, performs backups, failover and data replication. SSH root access to database instances is not available to tenants. Each database instance can contain multiple user created tables. Amazon RDS use Elastic Block Store (EBS) volumes for database and log storage. Allocated storage can be increased with multiple striped EBS volumes.

The data at rest is encrypted with AES256 cipher encryption. Amazon RDS creates an SSL certificate on the database instance automatically when it is created. These certificates are signed by a certificate authority. The SSL certificate includes the DB instance endpoint as the Common Name for SSL certificate to prevent spoofing attacks.

Read Replica

RDS enables horizontal scaling with read replicas that allow you to elastically scale out as database workloads increase. Multiple read requests are routed (split) among read replicas to improve throughput and lower latency for average and peak traffic events. Adding read replicas to an RDS managed database would increase database capacity through number of transactions per second. The effect of horizontal scaling is to distribute packets across multiple database instances. Read replicas are read-only copies that are synchronized with a source (master) database instance.

There is support as well for locating read replicas in a different AWS Region closer to customers or employees for minimizing latency. Any read replica can be promoted to a master for faster recovery in the event of a disaster. It is not an automatic failover however and not the optimal solution for fault tolerance that is available with Multi-AZ standby replica.

Amazon AWS supports copying EBS Snapshots between different regions. In addition tenants can create read replicas of an encrypted database to a different region. Any encrypted data remains encrypted while in transit as well.

Figure 18 Amazon RDS for MySQL Multi-AZ Replication

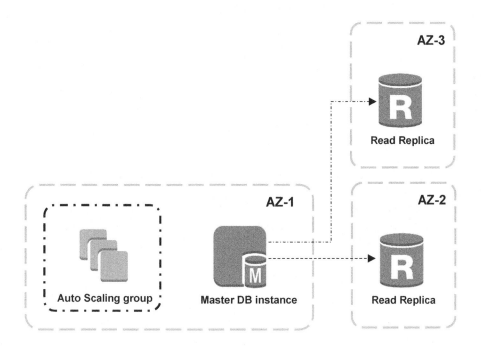

There is an RDS backup window that is configurable by tenants. It defines a time interval when AWS does a backup of data. The backup window is configured by tenants when creating a database instance. AWS assigns a default 30-minute backup window at random if the tenant does not assign a backup window. In addition there is a default backup window selected from an 8-hour block of time per region. RDS defaults the backup retention period to one day if configured using RDS API or the AWS CLI when not configured by the tenant. RDS defaults retention period to 7 days if configured from AWS console.

The source database is encrypted at rest and while in transit for read replications to slave databases within the cloud. Any read replication requires selecting a target region and encryption key for target region. You can use your own key or default key generated by KVM in the target region.

The source database sends only read-only replica updates after the initial synchronization to slave database/s has occurred. There is currently support for up to five in-region and cross-region replicas supported per API call. In addition Amazon permits a maximum of 40 RDS database instances.

Multi-AZ Standby Replica

The primary feature for fault tolerance is a standby replica that automatically provisions and maintains a synchronous standby replica in a different Availability Zone. The primary RDS database instance is synchronously replicated across Availability Zones to a standby replica. This is a key aspect of deploying fault tolerant systems with minimal to no downtime.

There is automatic failure detection and failover to the standby replica for disaster recovery purposes. The advantages are fault tolerance, data redundancy and eliminating I/O freezes to the hard drive subsystem. It makes system maintenance much easier as well when a standby replica is available during software maintenance windows.

Load Balancing

The native transparent load balancing is used to forward queries between all database instances that are assigned a unique DNS hostname making it an endpoint. Currently there is no support for deploying ELB with Amazon RDS. The recommended solution for advanced load balancing is AWS Application Load Balancer or HAProxy.

Database Migration Service (DMS)

Amazon AWS Database Migration Service (DMS) enables tenants to easily migrate an on-premises SQL database to Amazon AWS RDS managed service. The service is initiated from Amazon DMS console where source and destination endpoints are configured to replicate database to the cloud. There are additional settings as well that determine how the database is replicated including transformation rules, monitoring checks and logging. Identity and Access Management (IAM) security policies are configured by tenants based on their requirements. It is typically similar permissions and roles they have when the database was originally on-premises at the enterprise data center.

RDS Storage Types

Storage type and database instance type provide vertical capacity scaling when initiating Amazon RDS services for an application. Tenants can specify data storage type and provide a storage size (GB) when creating or modifying a database instance. The storage type assigned to your instance is changed as well by modifying the database instance. The options are Provisioned IOPS, General Purpose (SSD) or Standard (Magnetic). There is a fixed amount of IOPS assigned to General Purpose and Magnetic storage types based on storage size. Provisioned IOPS enables allocating an amount of dedicated IOPS (input/output operations per second) to a database instance. Magnetic storage type is still available for backward compatibility however not recommended for new deployments.

An immediate outage occurs when converting to a different storage type and data for that database instance is migrated to a new volume. Increasing the allocated storage however does not cause any outage. The database instances are assigned to an instance class (type) as well. The attributes include standard vCPU, memory and network throughput limits. In addition some instance types are EBS-optimized and IOPS optimized for maximum performance. Instances with EBS-optimized volumes do not share network bandwidth with other traffic.

Amazon RDS recently increased maximum database storage size up to 16 TB when using Provisioned IOPS and General Purpose (SSD) storage. Standard redundancy features include multiple availability zones (Multi-AZ) and read replication for scalability.

RDS creates a database instance with multiple database tables with assigned processing and volume disk size. The advantage of larger database size and higher IOPS is higher workloads on a single Amazon RDS instance without distributing the data across multiple instances.

RDS Use Case

❖ RDS is preferred for an online transaction processing (OLTP) application where there are significant workloads. The storage type recommended for transaction processing applications with large I/O intensive workloads is Provisioned IOPS. The IOPS rate and storage space allocation is selected from a range available by the tenant when the database instance is created. In addition you can allocate additional storage and/or convert to a different storage type at any time.

The database instance type used with database instances specifies capacity with number of IOPS and network throughput (Mbps). Amazon recommends a subset of instance types (M4,M3,R4,R3,M2) that are optimized for IOPS storage when the database is using Provisioned IOPS storage type. General Purpose (SSD) storage type is typically used for small to medium sized databases with moderate workloads and IOPS throughput requirements.

❖ You have enabled Amazon RDS database services in VPC1 for an application with public web servers in VPC2. How do you connect the web servers to the RDS database instance so they can communicate considering the VPC's are in different regions?

Any traffic sent between EC2 instances and/or AWS services in different regions (cross-region) must traverse the internet. Each VPC must have an Internet gateway in a public subnet and a default route in the custom route table to the Internet gateway.

EC2 instances for the web servers and the RDS database instance are assigned to a public subnet associated to a custom route table within each VPC. In addition, EC2 instances and database instance/s are assigned Elastic IP (EIP) addresses for internet access. It is preferable to use EIP instead of public IPv4 addresses for persistence. The database instance in VPC1 must allow public access. RDS automatically creates a public subnet for your database instance when selecting VPC option to create new VPC and Publicly Accessible option to Yes.

RDS for Microsoft SQL Server

RDS managed service support Microsoft SQL Server database mirroring and vertical scaling. Microsoft SQL Server primary database mirrors real-time data to a standby replication server for fault tolerance. Database requests are redirected to the standby server for failover only when the primary is not available. As a result only the warm standby service is available with SQL server for disaster recovery.

Amazon supports backup/restore of SQL server database instances to S3 storage as well. RDS provides vertical scaling of SQL database instances for increasing capacity. Tenants can increase allocated storage to the database instance and/or assign a larger instance type.

RDS for MySQL

There is support for real-time database replication with RDS for MySQL database instances and Multi-AZ failover. The master and standby replicas are assigned to different Availability Zones. The primary database server replicates data in real time to standby replicas. That allows the tenant to send read requests to the primary and replica database instances. That feature is not available with Microsoft SQL Server for RDS. In addition RDS manages failover to the replica during an outage. Database requests are redirected to the standby replica when the primary database is not available.

Amazon Aurora

Amazon Aurora is a cost-effective open source relational database that is fully managed by RDS. It is an enhancement of sorts to RDS that is MySQL and PostgreSQL compatible. It is five time faster than standard MySQL databases with faster recovery time and minimized replication lag. It provides the security, fault tolerance and durability of commercial databases at 10% of the cost.

Data Analytics

Elasticsearch

Amazon AWS Elasticsearch is a managed service for text search and document indexing. It is an open source analytical engine with use cases such as log analytics, real-time application monitoring and clickstreams.

The core services of Elasticsearch provide deployment and scaling of clusters (servers) for federated indexing and text search. The cluster is defined with a variety of configuration settings such as EBS volume, snapshots, redundancy, software version and VPC. There is support for instance store and EBS volumes for data storage and attaching to a VPC.

Redshift

RedShift is well suited for warehousing and analyzing Petabyte amounts of data to run SQL analytical tools. The purpose of RedShift is to provide a data warehouse solution where tenants can run sophisticated SQL queries and Business Intelligence reporting tools in real-time or offline. RedShift analyzes behaviors, patterns and trends for gaming, stocks, logs, twitter, sensor data and clickstreams.

Redshift Use Case

Your company is a provider of online gaming that customers access with various network access devices including mobile phones. Redshift is a data warehousing solutions for large amounts of information on player behavior, statistics and events for analysis using SQL tools. Online gaming applications generate TB+ amounts of data that can be analyzed and used for adding new features and optimize marketing strategies.

Elastic Map Reduce (EMR)

EMR enable tenants to run analytics on large data sets based on custom code for a variety of complex applications. Redshift by contrast is used for real-time and offline SQL queries only and business intelligence analytical reporting tools. RedShift data is structured while EMR can run analytics on unstructured data. There is additional cost associated with EMR so tenants would typically not run SQL queries with it for example.

ElastiCache

Data Store Caching

Amazon ElastiCache is a fast in-memory caching service. It allows tenants to store often accessed data from multiple data stores. The strategy offloads processing to optimize data access time. The result is much lower latency and response time that result in faster queries. There is less durability however when compared with native database access. Amazon AWS supports the popular Memcached and Redis caching engines. It is a managed service that offloads the deployment, maintenance and administration of caching software from tenants to the cloud.

ElastiCache is accessed through EC2 instances from the VPC where the ElastiCache instance was launched. ElastiCache instance can be accessed across a VPC peering link as well. Each instance is configured with an endpoint for connecting to ElastiCache services. Each node and cluster is assigned a unique address that creates an endpoint used to connect applications with caching services.

Figure 19 ElastiCache Operation

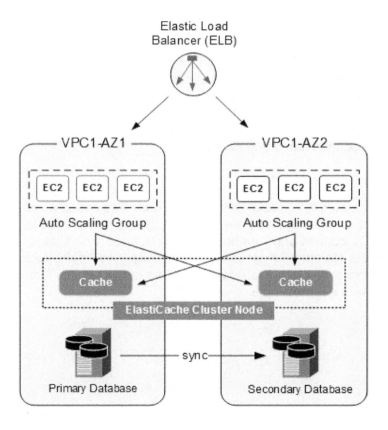

Cloud Operation

The cache stores a key-value pair that is much faster than running queries directly on a database. In addition previous results of complex queries are cached for fast access instead of repeating query. There is high performance response time and no charge for unnecessary queries making it cost effective.

Tenants are recommended to cache static content that is frequently accessed for optimized advantages. In addition determine the tolerance for staleness and what affect that has on your application ecosystem. Any content that changes often and not accessed as much is outdated faster and not suitable for caching. ElastiCache architecture does not provide the same level of durability as S3 for example however there is lower latency for data access. Redis caching engine supports replication with clusters for fault tolerance.

Caching Engines

ElastiCache clusters are comprised of multiple ElastiCache nodes running instances of Memcached or Redis caching engine. Each cluster must run the same caching engine on node instances within ElastiCache. There is no support for Memcached as persistence session store to enable stateful applications. It is a caching solutions only where the associated database would store stateful web session data for persistence. There is support however with Redis caching engine for that purpose.

Memcached architecture partitions tenant data across multiple nodes that create a cluster for horizontal scaling. The default support is from 1 to 20 nodes that can be added or removed. Scaling any Memcached cluster up or down requires the tenant to create a new cluster.

In-transit encryption is supported only for Redis replication groups running in an Amazon VPC. You can enable in-transit encryption on a replication group only when creating the replication group. In-transit encryption encrypts data when it is forwarded between replication group and application. In addition TLS must be the encryption protocol deployed on the database. AWS ElastiCache for Redis supports at-rest encryption when it is enabled on a replication group. The data is encrypted for all disk operations. The following features supported with Redis engine are not available with Memcached caching engine.

- redundant Multi-AZ asynchronous replication
- complex data objects (hash, list, sets)
- session persistence store for web-based applications

Fault Tolerant Systems

AWS Global Architecture

Amazon AWS is a global network topology comprised of multiple regions with multiple data centers called Availability Zones (AZ) per region. Availability Zones are inter-connected with private high speed redundant links within the region. There are high speed links as well that interconnect each region. The private links interconnecting Availability Zones forward traffic within the AWS cloud.

The purpose of Availability Zones is to enable high availability and fault tolerance for customer applications. Amazon AWS replicates subnets, EC2 instances, application data and cloud stacks across multiple availability zones. Some AWS services provide this as a native operational feature. The following table lists each AWS service and the support for global, regional and/or availability zone operational deployment.

Table 10 AWS Services Operational Deployment Classes

Global	Region	Availability Zone
• Route 53 • IAM • CloudFront • WAF	• AMI • VPC • Security Group • Auto Scaling • ELB • S3 • DynamoDB • NACL	• EC2 Instance • Subnet • EBS Volume • Placement Group

Most AWS services are regional-based where they reside in a single or multiple Availability Zones. There is support as well for deploying the same services cross- region. The services that are globally managed include Route 53, IAM, CloudFront and WAF. The tenant does not have to recreate or copy anything between regions to enable features or change configuration. IAM is a unified security schema that is not assigned to any particular region.

Scaling Concepts

Vertical scaling adds or decreases capacity available to a single EC2 instance based on the assigned instance type. The tenant would assign a higher instance type to add capacity and lower instance type to decrease capacity. Horizontal scaling adds or decreases capacity available to an Auto-Scaling group or database. The tenant can add or remove EC2 instances to an auto-scaling group. That would for instance permit additional user session connections per second to public web servers.

DNS Route 53

Route 53 is a scalable DNS service that enables resolving queries from internet sources to CloudFront, Elastic Beanstalk, ELB and S3. Amazon AWS manages a global network of authoritative DNS servers that route internet traffic at no charge. In addition customers can register domain names.

It is a reverse proxy service that manages DNS tables and redirects sessions to available endpoints. There is support for standard resource record types such as MX (mail), A (IP address), canonical name (CNAME) and Name Server (NS). Customers can configure load balancing between primary and failover locations for fault tolerance. Any global load balancing service such as Route 53 basically manages DNS records to affect where packets are forwarded. There is support for a variety of routing policies based on tenant requirements.

DNS Route 53 is a global load balancer that can load balance traffic to multiple Elastic Load Balancers. There is cross-region support for load balancing as a result that is available as well. Traffic can be forwarded to multiple availability zones at the same or different regions for Multi-Site failover and recovery. The tenant configures weighting for load balancing between multiple locations. DNS weighting can forward a percentage of tenant traffic to a VPC for example and some to a failover data center for global load balancing.

Health Checks

The health check starts with opening a TCP connection between route 53 and an endpoint with a DNS record to verify connectivity. The TCP connection is configurable based on TCP, HTTP or HTTPS protocols. You could for example configure a health check for some public web servers (HTTPS) stored on an S3 bucket. CloudWatch alarms can be configured as well to send SNS notification when an endpoint is not available.

There is routing of internet traffic away from unhealthy endpoints. The tenant adds health checks to all of the records in a group of weighted records. In addition there are nonzero weights assigned to all of the records for creating Multi-Site active/active failover.

DNS Route 53 cycles through each DNS record based on weight when a record fails health check. The healthy record is then used for responding to the DNS query with an IP address. Health checks are defined by an endpoint, protocol (HTTP, HTTPS,TCP), IP address and port to use for an instance.

Figure 20 DNS Route 53

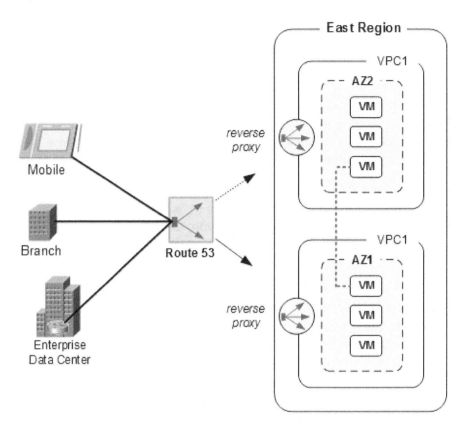

DNS Records

Based on standard DNS specifications, all (A) records resolve a hostname to an IP address. In addition the Alias record is a DNS extension that resolves a hostname to another hostname. The Alias record type is used specifically to alias the root domain (zone apex).

For example a zone apex is domain name cisconetsolutions.com (instead of subdomain www.cisconetsolutions.com). Tenants would use Alias Records within AWS to map a tenant zone apex in a hosted zone to either an ELB, CloudFront distribution, Beanstalk or S3 bucket of a tenant. An example is mapping tenant zone apex (yourwebapp.com) to another target such as Elastic Load Balancer DNS name (elb2345.elb.amazonaws.com).

DNS Alias records that point to CloudFront distribution, load balancer or S3 buckets use default TTL value of the AWS services (60 seconds). There is no default TTL for basic DNS records. It is configured based on a range that considers a variety of requirements such as application and cost.

The 'A' record for the ELB is then used to resolve the hostname to IP address of the ELB. The advantage of Alias records is faster update of DNS records when an IP address changes within the cloud. The hostnames often do not change when assigned to services. In addition it is easier for tenants and customers to use a custom zone apex instead of a complex lengthy Elastic Load Balancer DNS name.

CNAME is used to resolve a hostname to another hostname similar to an Alias. CNAME is typically used for subdomains where www.yourwebapp.com for example would resolve (point) to amazon.elb.aws.amazon.com (DNS name of ELB). The DNS 'A' record is then used to resolve amazon.elb.aws.amazon.com to its IP address.

CNAME is a DNS record type that permits tenants to use a domain name of their own for links to objects instead of using the domain name that AWS assigns. An example is the domain name that AWS assigns to CloudFront distributions. The CNAME cannot be used to create a record for your zone apex (root domain).

The tenant zone file includes DNS resource records (A, Alias, CNAME, MX, NS etc.) used by AWS Route 53 for resolving hostnames to IP addresses for servers and AWS services. Each tenant can manage configuration of DNS Route 53 services to enable internet access for applications, global load balancing and fault tolerant systems. The following describes DNS resolution with different record types when there is a request for a web page.

Example DNS Record Lookups:

Client makes request for a web page → DNS Route 53

A Record → amazon.elb.aws.amazon.com = 198.200.1.1

CNAME Record = www.yourwebapp.com = amazon.elb.aws.amazon.com → **A Record** → amazon.elb.aws.amazon.com = 198.200.1.1

ALIAS Record = yourwebapp.com = amazon.elb.aws.amazon.com → **A Record** → amazon.elb.aws.amazon.com = 198.200.1.1

RTO / RPO Design

Recovery Time Objective (RTO) is the time it takes after a disruption to restore services to normal based on an operational level agreement (OLA). Recovery Point Objective (RPO) is defined as the acceptable amount of data loss during the RTO period. Tenants should create fault tolerant systems with redundancy design that is based on RTO/RPO. The following are Amazon AWS fault tolerant systems designs with varying RTO/RPO levels.

Backup and Restore

This is based on data restore from backups that were made with bulk data transfer or a snapshot service to an S3 bucket. The tenant should as a minimum make backups of on-premises and cloud-based volumes. In addition Amazon auto-replicates data within an Availability Zone. It is a common practice for tenants to make EBS snapshots from EC2 instances. The backup and restore has the highest recovery time of all methods. The RPO = last snapshot and RTO = time to manually restore and start EBS volume.

Pilot Light

This method is based on locating the production application on-premises and duplicating minimal core components at AWS that are not active. There is real-time database replication to Amazon cloud across a Direct Connect link. The result is a lower RTO/RPO than backup method. RPO = minimal, RTO = time to start instances, failover and establish user sessions establish.

Warm Standby

This design is similar to Pilot Light however there are operational web and application servers at AWS running minimally and not processing traffic. The advantage is RTO/RPO is further minimized with a faster failover having AWS EC2 instances operational ready. Amazon AWS automates DNS route 53 traffic redirect to AWS data center with health checks or modify DNS records manually. In addition EC2 instances launch along with ELB and Auto-Scaling. There is a lower RTO/RTO than Pilot Light measured in minutes.

Multi-Site

This duplicates the production environment from on-premises to Amazon AWS cloud. DNS route 53 route policies are modified to load balance traffic between on-premises and AWS cloud. DNS route 53 is a global load balancer splitting traffic load between multiple location. There is real-time mirroring or data replication from on-premises database to a slave database in the cloud for database synchronization. The database platform determines whether mirroring or replication is recommended or available. Multi-site design has the lowest RTO and RPO where is near to no downtime.

Failover Records

You can create an active/passive failover configuration by using failover records. You create a primary and a secondary failover record that have the same name and type, and you associate a health check with each. The primary and secondary failover records can refer to anything from an Amazon S3 bucket that is configured as a website to a complex tree of records. When all of the resources that are referenced by the primary failover record are unhealthy, Amazon Route 53 automatically begins responding to queries by using the resources that are referenced by the secondary failover record.

Deployment/Orchestration

API Gateway

API gateway is platform used to publish and manage APIs used for calling (proxy) various AWS backend services. In addition it adds functionality to internet-based mobile and enterprise applications. It is a managed service that provides automatic scaling for capacity, cost effective usage and integration with Identity and Access Management (IAM). The following summarizes primary features of API gateway architecture.

- proxy to backend AWS services
- processes API calls
- does not run within VPC
- only supports public endpoints (HTTPS)
- charge only for API calls received and data transfer out.

Figure 21 API Gateway Architecture

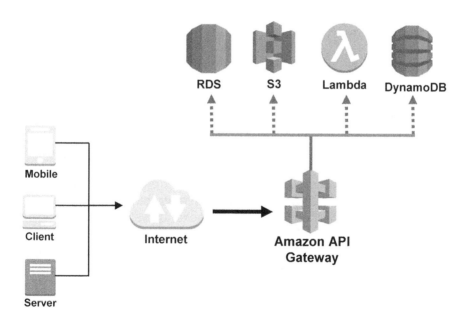

API gateway endpoints are web servers, AWS services or Lambda functions. The API integrates an HTTP method (GET, PUT, POST) operation with an endpoint. There is no support for unencrypted endpoints since they are external to the AWS cloud. The following are some added advantages of API gateway.

- automatic DDoS protection (SYN floods)
- caching API calls to prevent redundant calls to backend services
- leverage existing IAM and Cognito setup to authorize access to APIs

The tenant could create an API on the API gateway that invokes a Lambda function. The API call invokes (triggers) a Lambda function to execute some code. Lambda enables serverless architecture where the EC2 instances are dynamically provisioned. The tenant does not have to define any EC2 servers (instances). The Lambda function could for instance read, update or delete an item from a DynamoDB table or object from an S3 bucket.

The results are returned to the mobile application across the internet. API gateway provides access and leverages AWS services for applications while adding functionality. The following example creates a serverless application based on RESTful API configured on the API gateway. It is used to update a DynamoDB table with a service request from a client such as a cab.

1. Mobile client selects HTTPS endpoint (web page URL on S3 bucket) that calls a RESTful API

2. RESTful API on API gateway invokes (triggers) Lambda function

3. Lambda functions execute code that writes data to database and/or return confirmation to mobile client

Most network throughput within any data center occurs at backend database servers and storage. The use of API to configure, launch and manage AWS services is a key aspect of cloud operations. In fact programmability is based on some API calls to physical and virtual-based infrastructure. API Gateway throttles traffic during peak traffic events to backend systems. In addition the output of API calls are cached to prevent redundant request to backend systems. API gateway requests pass through to the backend service when caching is not enabled and throttling limits are reached until account level throttling limits are reached.

- API Gateway can communicate to multiple backends
- Lambda functions
- AWS Step functions state machines
- HTTP endpoints exposed through Beanstalk, ELB or EC2 instances
- Non-AWS hosted HTTP based operations accessible via public internet

Cross-Origin Resource Sharing (CORS)

For security reasons making HTTP requests (GET, PUT etc.) from within scripts (Java) is not permitted to a different domain (cross-domains) than the source domain where the web browser originated the request. There is support for CORS to permit S3 bucket as an origin to forward requests.

You can create an XML file with up to 100 rules and permit all origins to access objects in a bucket. Amazon S3 after receiving a preflight request from the web browser sends it to an XML file. CORS must be enabled on HTTP endpoints that connect to an API gateway when RESTful APIs are configured. CORS is a key feature that is supported with CloudFront operation and S3 buckets as well.

Simple Queue Service (SQS)

SQS is a hosted queuing service used to store messages sent between distributed application components. It enables associated applications to manage work items in a queue and track status to confirm delivery. In addition customers can enable individual message delay for up to 15 minutes. SQS as a managed service will scale automatically based on workload. The queue size is increased (scaled) automatically during peak loads. The number of read/write operations of messages supported is lower than Kinesis with batch operations.

There are only some regions that provide all of the available feature set. There is fault tolerance with multiple availability zone redundancy enabled as a default (native) feature with SQS. The following are key features of SQS architecture.

- fully managed message queuing service
- creates loosely coupled distributed applications
- priority queues supported
- poll-based
- automatic capacity scaling based on workloads

The queue service levels available with SQS include both standard and FIFO queuing. The standard queue stores all messages with maximum throughput and best-effort ordering. In addition there is at-least-one delivery service. First-in First-out (FIFO) queuing orders messages in the queue based on when they arrive. It is called sequencing and a feature required by some applications for processing messages. FIFO guarantees that messages are processed only once. There is a maximum of 300 transactions/sec. with a single FIFO queue.

The queue has a global **visibility timeout** setting that enables multiple readers (applications) to access the same queue so messages are not processed multiple times. It is configurable from the default setting of 30 seconds.

Kinesis Data Streams

Kinesis data streams is used to capture and store big data (TB/hr) streams from hundreds of sources such as application logs, location-tracking events or web transactions for example. You can configure Lambda to automatically poll your stream for example and process any new records.

- enable real-time processing of streaming big data
- routing, ordering and replay of records
- multiple clients can read messages from the same stream concurrently
- replay of messages up to seven days
- customer can consume records at a later time
- capacity is manually configured before activating stream

Kinesis Operation

Consumers are EC2 instances that process (include transform) data records and forward them to storage, database or Kinesis firehose platform for analysis. Consider for example the large scale amount of data that results from millions of remote wireless sensors sending real-time data to an application.

The consumers forward data to storage service such as S3 and/or database services such as RedShift or DynamoDB. The support for adding multiple consumers to a Kinesis data stream and record replay distinguishes Kinesis from SQS. Kinesis also synchronously replicates data across three Availability Zones for redundancy. Kinesis Streams will not automatically scale based on workload (add capacity). Configure enough streams initially for capacity requirements of data producers and data consumers.

Kinesis data stream starts with a producer that puts real-time data records into a Kinesis data stream. For example consider a web server that is sending log data to a Kinesis stream. The consumer is an EC2 instance that processes the data records in real-time from a Kinesis stream. Records from a stream are available for up to 24 hours by default however extended data retention enables access for up to 7 days. The data stream is processed by a single or multiple consumers running on EC2 instances.

Kinesis Record Structure

Kinesis data records are composed of a sequence number, partition key and data blob with a maximum payload size of 1 MB. The shard is a grouping of data records that form the basic element of a data stream. In addition tenants must specify the number of shards when defining a data stream. The capacity of a single shard is 1MB/sec data input and 2MB/sec data output that supports 1000 PUT records per second. The tenant can increase the number of shards to increase data stream capacity based on requirements.

Firehose

The primary purpose of Kinesis Firehose is to capture a Kinesis data stream and forward it to a supported storage platform. The tenant assigns an EC2 instance (consumer) that forwards a Kinesis stream to Kinesis firehose. The tenant can run Business Intelligence (BI) tools for analysis purposes on data loaded to RedShift for example.

The scale of data associated with a Kinesis data stream is massive. It enables tenants to run analytical tools and derive a lot of reports and associated results. Note that Firehose is essentially an intermediary to RedShift, S3, Elasticsearch and Splunk for delivery and transformation. There is server-side encryption at rest as well for data security.

Use Case

* ❖ The data written from Firehose or DynamoDB to RedShift for instance is typically used for real-time analysis of data. Application data from IoT sensors can be streamed through Kinesis data streams as well and saved to DynamoDB for store and retrieval purposes. There is no current support for directly moving DynamoDB streams to RDS. They are separate database platforms with different data structures. Data from Firehose originates from Kinesis streams.

Your company has developed an IoT application that sends Telemetry data from 100,000 sensors. The sensors send a datapoint of 1 KB at one-minute intervals to a DynamoDB collector for monitoring purposes. What AWS stack would enable you to store data for real-time processing and analytics using BI tools?

A. Sensors → Kinesis Data Streams → Firehose → DynamoDB → RDS

B. Sensors → Kinesis Data Streams → Firehose → DynamoDB → S3

C. Sensors → AWS IoT → Firehose → RedShift

D. Sensors → Kinesis Data Streams → Firehose → RDS

Answer (C)

Sensor datapoints are processed when they ingress to the cloud with AWS IoT or Kinesis data streams that can distribute the datapoint stream to a variety of AWS services. The purpose of RedShift is to provide a data warehouse solution where tenants can run sophisticated SQL queries and Business Intelligence reporting tools in real-time or offline. RedShift can analyze behaviors, patterns and trends for gaming, stocks, logs, twitter, sensor data and clickstreams.

Table 11 Kinesis Data Streams vs Firehose Comparison

Kinesis Streams	Firehose
Not managed	Fully managed
7-day store	Automatic scaling
Multiple AWS services	S3, Redshift, Elasticsearch, Splunk
Custom processing	Transform data for destination format
Low latency	Higher latency

The following are differences between Kinesis streams and Kinesis Firehose.

* Kinesis data streams capture, process and analyze streams
* Kinesis Firehose captures and loads Kinesis data stream to data store
* Kinesis data streams forwards traffic to consumers first

Lambda

Lambda is a new cloud architecture that now enables serverless computing. The cloud is currently based on the virtual machine as a building block. Tenants currently use a static model where an application is bundled into an AMI and assigned an EC2 instance. AWS enables developers to submit code with various supported platforms to Lambda. All server management, infrastructure provisioning, redundancy and orchestration is provided by Lambda.

In contrast to Beanstalk, tenants cannot access any EC2 instances or other cloud infrastructure generated by Lambda. It is abstracted so there is no control of AWS infrastructure. It is primarily used for adding functionality to applications and managing any AWS service. As a result it is further redefining how applications can be deployed and managed.

Lambda blocks all inbound (public internet) network connections and permits only TCP/IP based outbound connections. In addition all ptrace access is denied and TCP port 25 (anti-spam) is blocked.

Function

Lambda functions are increasingly used to enable complex application operations and data migration between multiple AWS services. Each AWS service has particular features that is used by Lambda functions to enable various store-transform-analyze processes for big data. The Lambda functions can read data from multiple sources including Kinesis streams, DynamoDB and S3. In addition Lambda can write to DynamoDB and S3 storage.

Tenants can upload code from any approved software platform as a Lambda function. The code written is stateless where any calls to files or hardware exists only for a single request. Each request is a new transaction and any associated stateful data is stored (persistent) on S3, DynamoDB or RDS.

Lambda stores tenant code in an S3 bucket where it is encrypted. Each function is allocated 500 MB of ephemeral (temporary) storage and maximum execution time is limited to 300 seconds. The maximum number of concurrent executions at any one time is 300. The default timeout is 3 seconds and configurable to between 1 and 300 seconds.

Event Source

Tenants configure AWS services or custom applications as event sources that publish events to automatically trigger or invoke a Lambda function. It is commonly known as event source mapping and defines Lambda operation. There is a subgroup of AWS services called stream services that include Kinesis and DynamoDB for Lambda functions.

Lambda functions are invoked by AWS services and events associated with operational state of AWS infrastructure. it is AWS services such as S3, DynamoDB or API gateway that are used to invoke a Lambda function.

CloudWatch events and SNS are used extensively as well based on operational state changes that can trigger Lambda functions. Cloud infrastructure such as EC2 instances and security groups are not services. They are however monitored for state changes and traffic forwarded to logs. You can write Lambda functions to process Amazon Simple Notification Service notifications. When a message is published to an Amazon SNS topic, the service can invoke your Lambda function by passing the message payload as parameter. Your Lambda function code can then process the event. For example publish the message to other SNS topics or send it to other services.

The event source mapping is configured to associate a source event with a Lambda function. The Lambda function defined in the bucket notification configuration is triggered when an event is detected such as a user copying a file to an S3 bucket. The Lambda function verifies security permissions before executing it on AWS services.

The S3 bucket is the event source that must be granted permissions to invoke the Lambda function. In addition the IAM role permissions you assigned to Lambda when the function was created is inherited by the Lambda function. The role permissions must allow access to the S3 bucket to run the function.

The primary difference between AWS services and streams-based event sources is where event source mapping is enabled. The event source mapping for AWS services is located at the event source (S3, Glacier, SNS, RDS etc.). The event source mapping for streams-based DynamoDB and Kinesis are maintained in AWS Lambda. It is a pull model where Lambda polls a stream for specific records and invokes a Lambda function when detected.

Versioning

The purpose of versioning is to maintain multiple versions of a function. Each AWS Lambda function has a single, current version of the code. There is native support for versioning of the same function within Lambda service. Tenants can leverage Aliases feature as well that act as a pointer to a function instead of using the assigned Amazon Resource Name (ARN).

The advantage of Aliases is managing software development and updates for production and testing. It is easier to use an Alias and point it to the Lambda function that is most current instead of all configuration updates required on the event source. Any published Lambda function cannot be changed (immutable) and as a result version and file management is a key aspect of Lambda service.

CloudFront

Amazon CloudFront is a global content delivery network (CDN) service with multiple regional edge locations. It provides web content from edge locations for the sole purpose of minimizing latency and maximizing throughput. As a result page loads are faster for web-based applications with less latency. CloudFront is based on pay-as-you-go pricing model with no initial fees. There is integrated WAF at each edge location as well for malware packet inspection. The following are primary advantages of migrating web content to CloudFront.

- global network infrastructure with elastic capacity
- maintains copies of objects in multiple edge locations globally
- persistent connections with origin servers to lower latency

Origin Servers

Origin servers reside at AWS where tenants copy original versions of web page content and media files called objects. The origin server for HTTP content is either an S3 bucket or a web server. The web server can run on an EC2 instance or privately managed server. In addition an elastic load balancer is a custom origin as well.

Any source that is not an S3 bucket is a custom origin. If the content is already in the edge location with the lowest latency, CloudFront delivers it immediately. If the content is not in that edge location, CloudFront retrieves it from an Amazon S3 bucket or an HTTP server (web server) that you have identified as the source for the definitive version of your content.

Figure 22 Amazon AWS Global CloudFront Distribution (CDN)

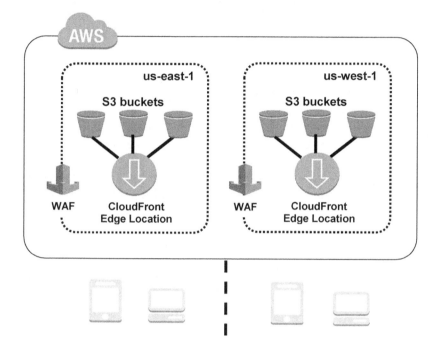

For example, CloudFront forwards request for image files to an S3 bucket (origin server) when not available at the edge location. Any requests for HTML files not at the edge location are forwarded to the origin HTTP (web) server. By default each object is cached in an edge location for 24 hours. After that a new request is required to copy object from origin server to an edge location where it is cached again.

Web Distributions

The tenant must configure CloudFront web distributions that are used by CloudFront to identify origin servers where objects are stored and any logging options. In addition there is a domain name assigned to a new distribution. CloudFront sends the distribution configuration file to all edge locations that are caching content for the tenant. Media files require a web distribution for media player and an RTMP distribution for the media files (on demand streaming).

The client starts with a requests to a web server or application owned by the AWS tenant. DNS routes the request to the nearest CloudFront edge location where latency is minimized (least number of hops). CloudFront then checks the edge location cache for the required objects that typically comprise a web page.

Origin Access Identity (OAI)

Origin Access Identity prevents users from accessing S3 objects with Amazon S3 URLs. It is a solution particularly applicable where HTTP web servers are hosting content for a web-based application. The following are steps required by tenants to enable OAI for their application.

1. Create a special CloudFront user called an origin access identity from the CloudFront console or API.

2. Give the origin access identity permission to read objects in your bucket. The user account is a proxy for access and retrieves objects for them.

3. Remove permissions for users to access Amazon S3 URLs to read objects. The user is denied access to objects based on an Amazon S3 URL and cannot bypass CloudFront security or infrastructure.

In addition to CloudFront security, OAI also mitigates the effects of any distributed denial of service attack (DDoS). SYN floods are a common DDoS that exploit the TCP three-way handshake. Any user requests are forwarded through CloudFront (and AWS) security where there is security enabled instead of S3 public access endpoints. That minimizes the attack surface to a private security managed infrastructure.

Signed URLs and Signed Cookies

The features that prevent users from bypassing CloudFront (and by extension AWS) security is CloudFront signed URLs and signed cookies. The private content in S3 buckets is accessed with CloudFront URLs provided to select users. The signed attributes include restrictions for users as part of defined security requirements. That permits security controls on content permitted by select users and charges where applicable. One part of a signed URL or cookie is hashed and signed using the private key from a public/private key pair. CloudFront compares signed and unsigned portions of the URL or cookie provided by user to grant access.

The request is denied when they don't match. There is supports for various origin servers and custom origin servers as part of a content solution. HTTP server is a custom origin server with objects that must be publicly accessible. As a result public objects are available to anyone who has the object URL without logging on or paying for the content. The purpose of OAI is to prevent unauthorized users from accessing objects with an S3 (public) URL.

CloudFront distributes media files on demand using the Adobe Media Server RTMP protocol from an S3 bucket (origin server) only. Any objects distributed from an S3 bucket can be either public or private read-only. Public content is available to anyone that knows the CloudFront URL. The objects set as private are only available when the signed URL or signed cookies are provided to the user. In addition the users must access private content with CloudFront URLs instead of Amazon S3 URLs for security purposes.

Use Case

❖ Your company is deploying a web site with dynamic content to customers in US, EU and APAC regions of the world. Content will include live streaming videos to customers. SSL certificates are required for security purposes.

CloudFront Content Delivery Network (CDN) can distribute web-based content to customers. It supports delivering dynamic web content that is cached to edge locations around the world. Caching web content locally to each region minimizes latency to customers and data transfer costs. There is support for deploying web endpoints with SSL certificates. By contrast, S3 is only suitable for static web content and does not support SSL certificates. There is higher latency and costs for remote access from multiple regions. CloudFront stores content in an S3 bucket as an origin server however content is cached to edge locations.

Beanstalk

Beanstalk is a managed service that translates application developer code to Amazon AWS services. It isolates the developer from having to know deployment specifics and provide requirements through code. The requests could include anything from fault tolerant systems to data warehousing. Beanstalk is suitable for deploying and scaling web applications and services developed with Java, .NET, PHP, Node.js, Python, Ruby, Go and Docker on servers such as Apache, Nginx, Passenger, and IIS. The tenant maintains full control over AWS infrastructure and can access the underlying instances.

CloudFormation

CloudFormation enables tenants to replicate an existing stack to a template (JSON script) with CloudFormer feature. That allows tenants for example to duplicate the same stack configuration to a different region. An AWS stack is comprised of all EC2 instances, AWS services and configuration associated with an application. That could include EC2 instances, Auto-Scaling, ELB, DynamoDB and Kinesis for example.

There is a significant work required to replicate the same configuration through AWS management console. In addition you have to remember all settings and options that were enabled. CloudFormer can create a new template from existing infrastructure with customized settings such as bucket names and addressing that is unique.

Use Cases

❖ You are a cloud engineer with JSON scripting experience and asked to select an AWS solution that enables automated deployment of cloud services. The template design would include a nondefault VPC with EC2 instances, ELB, Auto-Scaling and active/active failover.

CloudFormation enables programmable infrastructure based on a JSON or YAML template that automates deployment of cloud services. The tenant creates a JSON template for instance for a fault tolerant database application. That requires EC2 instances for all servers associated with the application. In addition storage is added and required services such as ELB, Auto-Scaling, CloudFront and DNS route 53. The failover RTO/RPO required determines how the stacks are configured.

❖ Your company has an application that was developed and migrated to AWS cloud. The application leverages EC2 instances, RDS database, S3 buckets, RedShift and Lambda functions. In addition there is IAM security with defined users, groups and roles. The application is monitored with CloudWatch and STS was recently added for permitting Web Identity Federation sign-on from Google accounts. You want a solution that can leverage the experience of your employees with AWS cloud infrastructure as well. What AWS service can create a template of the design and configuration for easier deployment of the application to multiple regions?

CloudFormation enables tenants to develop templates based on YAML or JSON scripting for deploying stacks to AWS cloud. It is a service that is oriented to tenants that understand AWS infrastructure components. The AWS service makes deployment easier considering it leverages the script where configuration and components are specified. Tenants can then duplicate the stack to a different region, make modifications where applicable and maintain a template for similar deployments.

OpsWorks

OpsWorks is a service that automates configuration and management of cloud environment. It supports Chef recipe scripts that automate cloud deployment tasks. It is often integrated with CloudFormation to provide operational, configuration and modeling services for cloud infrastructure.

Elastic Container Service

EC2 Container Services (ECS) enable easier deployment of Docker-based containers. It is an alternate architecture to virtual machines. The container requires only minimum operating system files shared by multiple applications. Tenants can run multiple container instances on a single or multiple EC2 instances. Complex applications use less memory and CPU usage.

Containerization is a dynamic model where tenants create containers for operating system virtualization. AWS manages deployment and orchestration of containers that are scalable and run on any hardware or operating system. EC2 Container Services enables easier deployment of Docker-based containers to the cloud. Containers are an alternate architecture to virtual machines.

The container is abstracted from the underlying operating system as a result making it lighter and portable within the cloud. The advantages of Elastic Container Service is easier deployment and orchestration of tenant containers that are less costly, scalable and redundant. The tenant only has to create the containers and select parameters for deployment to AWS.

Microservices architecture decouples a single application into multiple services that are connected through light APIs. The software development and management approach is decentralized where separate teams are assigned to services. The isolation of services creates more stable, fault tolerant and easier to manage applications. In addition any errors or performance problems are isolated to a single service and do not affect other services. Application Load Balancer and ECS are key to enabling Microservices.

Stateless Systems

Stateless applications do not save any session information when a transaction ends. An example of a stateless protocol is HTTP. The stateless application sends a group of requests to a web server where the session data (not the application data) is deleted from cache when the browser starts a new connection. Stateful applications cache session data for clients that is used for multiple transactions during the course of a session for fault tolerance.

Amazon AWS cloud is comprised of multiple instances. The tenant can deploy a stateless web-based application and leverage databases such as RDS that can be used to save session information. The ELB would redirect a user session to an available web server for instance when there is a web server failure from an Auto-Scaling group. The web server would query the associated database and retrieve session information. That enables stateful behavior with the associated advantages of elasticity and fault tolerance particularly where ElastiCache is deployed for caching application and session state data.

Monitoring Services

CloudWatch

CloudWatch is the monitoring platform that is integrated with AWS services. It is used for monitoring operational status and performance metrics within the cloud. Amazon CloudWatch is designed to collect and track metrics, monitor log files and set alarms. It can be accessed from AWS console, CLI or API calls. AWS monitoring is based on hypervisor-level performance metrics. Any application level or operating system level metrics are the responsibility of customer.

Metrics

Metric is a time-ordered set of data points published to CloudWatch. The metrics for each application are assigned to containers (namespaces) that isolate results for accurate reporting.

- UTC time zone is the default
- metric comprised of unique name, namespace, and dimension/s
- each data point has a time stamp and a unit of measure (optional)
- data points are custom metrics or metrics from other services in AWS

Alarms

CloudWatch alarms each monitor a single metric over a specified time interval and takes some action/s based on the value of the metric with a predefined threshold and time interval. CloudWatch provided support for sending a notification (action) to an EC2 Auto Scaling policy, SNS topic or an EC2 instance. There is standard support for creating dashboards and adding alarms similar to traditional monitoring software. Alarms are created and apply to a single region only. In addition the alarm history is available for only 14 days.

Alarm States

OK = metric is within the defined threshold

ALARM = metric is outside of the defined threshold

INSUFFICIENT_DATA = alarm is in startup, metric is not available or not enough data exists for the metric to determine an alarm state

Example Actions:

- detect and shut down EC2 instances that are unused or underutilized
- stop, start, or terminate EC2 instance based on utilization
- notify Auto Scaling policy or change state

EC2 Auto-Scaling

CloudWatch alarms can be used to monitor CPU and memory thresholds for EC2 instances assigned to an Auto-Scaling group. Additional EC2 instances can be added to the Auto-Scaling group when performance thresholds are exceeded.

There is a cool down setting available with Auto-Scaling that specifies a minimum time before adding or releasing EC2 instances. The purpose is to stabilize operational state and prevent performance issues from adding or terminating instances too fast during periods of changing workloads.

CloudWatch Operation

CloudWatch monitors data created by applications and systems messages that are sent to their log files. The log data is analyzed based on metrics and used to generate a CloudWatch log file. The results of alarms can be used to send email notifications or rules-based changes to AWS services.

Figure 23 AWS Monitoring Architecture

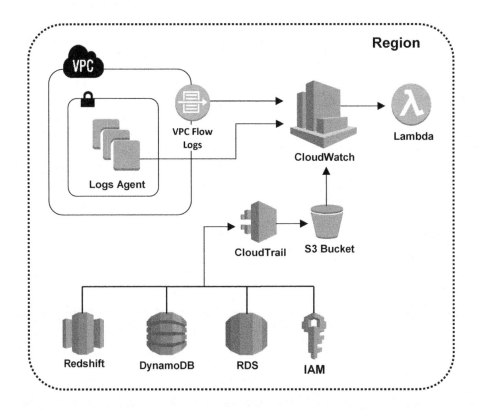

VPC Flow Logs monitor all ingress and egress IP traffic on network interfaces. Customized alarms are used for specific events. That could include for instance when packets are denied or certain traffic types detected. CloudTrail log events and VPC Flow Logs are stored in Cloudwatch Log files for analysis and review. IAM user and IP address that made the network access attempts or policy changes can be identified from CloudWatch logs. EC2 instances for servers generate operating system and application generated log files.

CloudWatch Logs Agent are enabled on each EC2 instance to create a log stream that publishes logs to CloudWatch Logs. There are a standard group of supported metrics generated by DynamoDB and RDS database instances that are sent automatically to CloudWatch. By contrast, alarms are configured by the tenant within CloudWatch based on requirements and CloudWatch support.

CloudTrail, VPC Flow Logs and Route 53 create logs directly accessible to CloudWatch. Each AWS service is granted sufficient permissions with an IAM role to publish logs to the specified log group in CloudWatch Logs. For example EC2 instances are accessed by tenants with SSH/RDP connections. Any errors including retry attempts and access denied is sent to a CloudWatch log

Basic Monitoring

The resolution for basic monitoring is every 5 minutes with some exceptions. and detailed monitoring is 1 minute resolution. That is the sample interval for polling metrics and alarms. Tenants must configure an alarm the polling interval that is equal to or greater than polling interval. High-resolution metrics permit high-resolution alarm with a period of 10 seconds or 30 seconds. Sample metrics include CPU utilization, disk read/write, network I/O, status checks AWS basic monitoring is free and enabled automatically for the following AWS services and features as a default:

EC2 instances, EBS volumes, Elastic Load Balancers, Auto Scaling groups, RDS instances, DynamoDB tables, ElastiCache clusters, RedShift clusters, OpsWorks stacks, Route 53 health checks, SNS topics, SQS queues, SWF workflows, Storage Gateways and EMR job flows.

- maximum of seven pre-selected metrics at 5 minute resolution
- maximum of three status check metrics at 1 minute resolution
- Auto Scaling, ELB and DNS Route 53 (1 minute resolution)
- customer cannot delete metrics until they expire
- Elastic Load Balancer – request count and latency
- data aggregation of metrics is per region only

Data Retention

There is a 15 month retention period storage of monitoring data even with service termination.

- data remains available for 15 days with 1-minute resolution
- after 15 days this data is aggregated and with resolution of 5 minutes
- after 63 days, the data is further aggregated with a resolution of 1 hour

Detailed Monitoring

Amazon AWS detailed monitoring is billed per feature and offers higher resolution (sample interval for datapoints) and custom metrics.

- same metrics as basic monitoring at 1 minute resolution
- regional data aggregation for AMI ID and instance type
- same retention period as basic monitoring
- high resolution custom metrics (1 second)
- high resolution for alarms (10 seconds)

Events

Amazon CloudWatch provide monitoring of AWS services for changes in operational status defined with an Event. AWS services such as EC2 instance for example generate an event when instance state changes that is published to CloudWatch Events. The rule/s are defined and associated with an event that triggers an action when a match occurs and routed it to a target for some action. For example activating functions, making changes or logging state information.

- Event Source = AWS service name and event pattern

- Event Type = Specific event to trigger rule match

- Target = AWS service to take some action when event occurs

- IAM Role = Assign permission to event allowing route to target

Event Source → Event Type → Add Target → Attach IAM Role

CloudWatch events can be used to schedule automatic EBS snapshots at selected intervals. That is recommended for restoring an EBS volume with minimal data loss. The IAM events role is created and assigned from the console allowing CloudWatch to make EBS snapshot. The tenant creates a CloudWatch events rule that triggers on an event.

Use Cases

❖ CloudWatch monitors and can send alerts when CloudTrail configured
events such as security violations occur. For instance SNS notifications
can be sent to tenant groups for a variety of CloudTrail events such as
authentication attempts or security rule changes when IAM security
policies are modified.

CloudWatch can send a message for instance to an SNS Topic that
triggers an event for a Lambda function. CloudTrail is an audit service
that generates logs for a variety of events and activities, stores them in
an S3 bucket and generate CloudWatch event that writes log files to an
S3 bucket. Each log file contains one or more records.

❖ Lambda functions are automatically monitored through Lambda service
and a log file is created for each function. There is real-time reporting of
cloud metrics through CloudWatch that include total requests, latency,
error rates and throttled requests.

Permissions

The tenant can configure and grant permissions to monitor various alarms,
create events and monitor logs. CloudWatch architecture is based on monitoring
application and operating system logs generated by EC2 instances.

CloudWatch user permissions are granted per feature and not per individual
AWS resources. For example enabling read-only access to alarms, metrics and
logs would apply to all AWS services for that user account. CloudWatch policies
are attached to the IAM user permissions. It is called identity-based policies
instead of resource-based policies.

CloudTrail

The function of CloudTrail is to provide an audit trail of all transactions
associated with an AWS account. That includes all users, what they accessed
and when it occurred. It is a catch-all monitoring service designed specifically to
monitor, record and log all API calls to and between all entities. It is important to
know who is using your AWS account services for transactions such as sign-on,
changing security settings and deleting volumes.

CloudTrail provides reporting that is used primarily for security compliance
requirements and optimizing security posture. The log files generated are
integrated with CloudWatch for analysis and reporting. For example CloudTrail
would log the API call when a user creates a Snapshot of a security sensitive
database or deletes an instance.

You can configure an SNS notification to notify you of the transaction. The log includes account username, API call and source IP address for audit purposes. Any audit trail is a key aspect of effective troubleshooting as well knowing when any recent change were made and who made it.

There are a variety of monitoring features available for EC2 instances, AWS services (ELB, Route 53 etc.) and database instances (DynamoDB, RDS etc). Each entity creates metrics, alarms and log files for analysis, troubleshooting and audit purposes. Rules-based alerts are supported as well that are designed to alert staff when a transaction is not permitted or potentially affects network security.

Simple Notification Service (SNS)

SNS is integrated with CloudWatch and CloudTrail for sending alerts and publishing alerts to a variety of AWS services. For example there is S3 bucket event notification that is used to send an SNS notification when a new video file is stored to an S3 bucket.

Simple Notification Service (SNS) supports SQS, Lambda, HTTP URL, email and SMS as subscriber endpoints for SNS. The tenant creates SNS topics and adds subscribers to enable notifications. Only standard SQS queues (no FIFO) are currently supported.

VPC Flow Logs

The purpose of flow logs is to capture IP traffic on network interfaces for analysis and troubleshooting. Security rules for instance are listed in flow logs along with any blocked traffic. The logs are stored and retrieved from Amazon CloudWatch service. VPC Flow Log do not capture real-time log streams for network interfaces.

Flow log data is published to a log group in CloudWatch Logs and each network interface has a unique log stream. After creating a flow log, you can view and retrieve its data in Amazon CloudWatch Logs.

Flow logs are often enabled for troubleshooting and resolving why packets are not arriving at an EC2 instance. That could be associated for example with incorrect security group rules. You can also use flow logs as a security tool to monitor the traffic that is reaching your instance. There is no additional charge for using flow logs however standard CloudWatch Logs charges apply.

You can create and attach a flow log to a VPC, subnet, or network interface. Attaching a flow log to a subnet enables monitoring of all network interfaces in that subnet. In addition attaching a flow log to a VPC enables monitoring of all network interfaces for all EC2 instances in the VPC.

To create a flow log:

- specify the resource for assigning and creating the flow log
- specify type of traffic to capture (accepted, dropped or all traffic)
- create log group name in CloudWatch Logs to publish
- assign ARN of an IAM role with publish permissions to CloudWatch Logs

You can create multiple flow logs that publish data to the same log group in CloudWatch Logs. If the same network interface is present in one or more flow logs in the same log group, it has one combined log stream. There is a new log stream created for each new network interface when subnet or VPC flow logs are configured. You can create flow logs for network interfaces that are created by other AWS services (Elastic Load Balancing etc.). Amazon AWS does not support resource tag feature for a flow log. The flow log displays the primary private IPv4 address in the destination IP address field.

Trusted Advisor

Trusted Advisor is an assessment tool that identifies common security misconfigurations and vulnerabilities. There are suggested best practices as well for improving system performance based on current utilization of EC2 instance for example.

Monitoring of service limits is available that notify tenants when to increase AWS resources. Trusted Advisor metrics in Amazon CloudWatch allow customers to create customizable alarms for individual service limits such as *EC2 On-Demand Instance* limits. Trusted Advisor forwards *ServiceLimitUsage* metric that represents the percentage of utilization versus the limit.

AWS Services Matrix

AWS Certified Solutions Architect Associate exam requires candidates to select solutions and answer questions based on use cases. In fact there are a significant number of questions that test knowledge of AWS services. That includes architecture, designing cloud solutions, integrating enterprise applications and security features. The following is a quick reference for students that describes considerations for selecting AWS services. In addition there is a solutions matrix with use cases for popular AWS services. Any cloud solution starts with defining common requirements and using that to select suitable AWS services.

Data Types?

data payload size, SQL, NoSQL, HTTP, SSL, text, static, dynamic, JSON, images

Throughput and Latency?

IOPS, requests per second, read/write per second, interface speed, latency, jitter, packet loss

Architecture?

serverless, API gateway, EC2, containers, multi-region

Storage Requirements?

persistent, ephemeral, file size, monthly, file system, latency, frequent access, restore features, cost, durability, service limits

Database Requirements?

table structure, query support, reporting, capacity, backups, snapshots, redundancy

Security Schema?

VPC, IAM policies, web identity federation, STS, firewalls, Cognito, data encryption, SSL certificates, WAF, security assessment, AD Connector

Monitoring?

alarms, metrics, alerts, audit, log management

Cloud Stack Configuration

Tenants create cloud stacks based on the requirements for an application. The solution (stack) is comprised of AWS services and configuration settings. The tenant should consider the following when creating a cloud stack.

selection = architecture + features + cost + performance + scalability + security

Full Stack Configuration

Compute + Storage + Database + Security + Monitor + Analytics + Deployment

Sample Use Case Cloud Stacks

Stack 1 = EC2 instances + ELB + Auto-Scaling + S3 (File Sharing)

Stack 2 = EC2 instances + ELB + Auto-Scaling + RDS (E-Commerce)

Stack 3 = EC2 instances + ELB + Auto-Scaling + DynamoDB + S3 (Bookstore)

Stack 4 = API Gateway + S3 + Lambda + DynamoDB (Mobile Services)

Stack 5 = EC2 + Kinesis Streams + Firehose + DynamoDB + RedShift (IoT)

Example: Multi-Tier Web Based Application

EC2 Compute = ELB + Auto-Scaling Group + EC2 Instances
Storage = S3
Database = DynamoDB
Security = VPC + IAM + STS + Firewall + Inspector
Monitoring = CloudWatch + CloudTrail + VPC Logs
Analytical = Elasticsearch + RedShift
Deployment = CloudFormation

Table 12 Solutions Matrix for AWS Services

AWS Service	Domain	Description	Use Case
EC2 Instance	Compute	Applications	Web servers Virtual appliances
Elastic Load Balancer	Compute	VPC load balancer Health checks Internet endpoint	Fault tolerance EC2 instances Multi-AZ Layer 4 (CLB, NLB) Layer 7 (ALB)
Auto-Scaling	Compute	EC2 instance group Manage capacity	Fault tolerance Horizontal scaling Multi-AZ
ECS	Compute	Fully managed Containerization Serverless	Docker Microservices Batch workloads Enterprise apps. Machine learning
Route 53	Compute	Global load balancer	Fault tolerance Disaster recovery Distribute workload Multi-region
S3	Storage	Multi-purpose Object level Auto-scalable Large file size Lower latency	Frequent access Any file format Snapshots Static web content Log files On-premises data
EBS	Storage	EC2 instances Database instances	Application data Persistent store
Glacier	Storage	Multi-purpose Archival service Large file size Higher latency	Infrequent access S3 archival On-premises data Security compliance

AWS Service	Domain	Description	Use Case
AWS Storage Gateway	Storage	Hybrid data store On-premises access Multiple store models Files, volumes, VTL	On-premises link to storage Apps. access cloud storage Lower latency to cloud S3, EBS, Glacier
Elastic File Storage (EFS)	Storage	File system mount EC2 instances NFSv4 protocol	File servers in the cloud Clients that support NFSv4 Emulate directory structure
RDS	Database	Relational database SQL-based queries Multi-AZ Automatic scaling	Fully managed service Administrative offload E-commerce Gaming app. database Oracle ERP
DynamoDB	Database	NoSQL Multiple data models Fast record lookups Automatic scaling In-memory caching	Fully managed service IoT sensor data Application log files Online service requests Indexing Store data streams
Aurora	Database	SQL database RDS Enhancements Clusters	Fully managed Faster recovery time Minimize replication lag
ElastiCache	Database	In-memory cache Faster queries Auto-scalable Redis/Memcached	Multiple databases Online gaming Stock transactions IoT applications
Snowball	Migration	Portable storage Appliance-based Data encryption at rest	Migrate more than 10 TB of on-premises data to S3
AWS Import/Export	Migration	Portable storage Appliance-based Data encryption at rest	Migrate less than 16 TB of on-premises data to S3 or EBS volume

AWS Service	Domain	Description	Use Case
RedShift	Analytic	Fully managed Petabyte data warehouse Complex SQL queries Multi-cluster scaling	Large datasets Real-time analytics BI reporting tools
EMR	Analytic	Fully managed Customized code Map reduce processing Expensive	Large scale datasets Log analysis Machine learning Data transform (ETL)
Elasticsearch	Analytics	Fully managed Search engine Index and query	Text-based search Log analytics Large data sets
Kinesis Streams	Analytic	Fully managed Cloud ingress point Process data streams Analyze and forward Multiple data sources	IoT sensors Clickstreams Stock transactions Gaming statistics
Kinesis Firehose	Analytic	Fully managed Capture data streams Transform data Forward to store	IoT sensor telemetry Transform/Load to S3 Load to RedShift Load to Elasticsearch
SQS	Messaging	Fully managed Message queuing Poll-based	Integrate applications Add functionality Event-triggered
CloudFront	Deployment	Content delivery network Web-based content Caching service Global customers	Global customers Web-based apps. File sharing Minimize latency
API Gateway	Deployment	Fully managed Application gateway AWS access point	Serverless Mobile applications Microservices
CloudFormation	Deployment	Template-based YAML / JSON scripting Deploy AWS services	Create, modify and standardize cloud stacks

AWS Service	Domain	Description	Use Case
OpsWorks	Deployment	Fully managed Configuration tool Chef recipes	Automate and update cloud configuration and deployments
Beanstalk	Deployment	Fully managed Translation service Multiple code platforms	Abstracts tenant from AWS services for deployments
SNS	Monitoring	Fully managed Notification service Push-model	Add functionality
CloudWatch	Monitoring	Umbrella service for cloud monitoring	EC2 instance logs VPC logs CloudTrail Basic/custom metrics
CloudTrail	Monitoring	AWS account monitoring	API calls Security compliance Troubleshooting

*** AWS Certification Practice Test ***

Test your knowledge with this sample test for AWS Certified Solutions Architect Associate exam. It is comprised of 60 selected questions and a time limit of 80 minutes. Each question is assigned one point and passing score is 70%.

- Read each question carefully and select the correct answer/s from the options provided. Use a pencil or erasable marker to select your answers.

- The answer key for the sample test is available after exam for you to verify your answers and tabulate results.

Question 1:

What are the minimum components required to enable a web-based application with public web servers and a private database tier? (Select three)

A. Internet gateway

B. Assign EIP addressing to database instances on private subnet

C. Virtual private gateway

D. Assign database instances to private subnet and private IP addressing

E. Assign EIP and private IP addressing to web servers on public subnet

Question 2:

What are supported features of CloudWatch operation? (Select two)

A. CloudWatch does not support custom metrics

B. CloudWatch permissions are granted per feature and not AWS resource

C. collect and monitor operating system and application generated log files

D. AWS services automatically create logs for CloudWatch

E. CloudTrail generates logs automatically when AWS account is activated

Question 3:

What Amazon AWS service is available for container management?

A. ECS

B. Docker

C. Kinesis

D. Lambda

Question 4:

What storage type is recommended for an online transaction processing (OLTP) application deployed to Multi-AZ RDS with significant workloads?

A. General Purpose SSD

B. Magnetic

C. EBS volumes

D. Provisioned IOPS

Question 5:

What class of EC2 instance type is recommended for database servers?

A. memory optimized

B. compute optimized

C. storage optimized

D. general purpose optimized

Question 6:

What three fault tolerant features are supported for S3 storage services?

A. cross-region replication

B. versioning must be disabled

C. cross-region asynchronous replication of objects

D. synchronous replication of objects within a region

E. multiple destination buckets

Question 7:

What is required to enable application and operating system generated logs and publish to CloudWatch Logs?

A. Syslog

B. enable access logs

C. IAM cross-account enabled

D. CloudWatch Log Agent

Question 8:

What are two advantages of cross-region replication of an S3 bucket?

A. cost

B. security compliance

C. scalability

D. Beanstalk support

E. minimize latency

Question 9:

What cloud compute (EC2 instances) components are configured by tenants and not Amazon AWS? (Select three)

A. hypervisor

B. upstream physical switch

C. virtual appliances

D. guest operating system

E. applications and databases

F. RDS

Question 10:

You have an Elastic Load Balancer assigned to a VPC with public and private subnets. ELB is configured to load balance traffic to a group of EC2 instances assigned to an Auto-Scaling group. What three statements are correct?

A. load balancer is assigned to a public subnet

B. network ACL is assigned to load balancer

C. security group is assigned to load balancer

D. cross-zone load balancing is not supported

E. load balancer forwards traffic to primary private IP address (eth0 interface) on each EC2 instance

Question 11:

What two features are supported with EBS volume Snapshot feature?

A. EBS replication across regions

B. EBS multi-zone replication

C. EBS single region only

D. full snapshot data only

E. unencrypted snapshot only

Question 12:

You have some developers working on code for an application and they require temporary access to AWS for up to an hour. What is the easiest AWS solution to provides access and minimize security exposure?

A. ACL

B. security group

C. IAM group

D. Security Token Service (STS)

E. EFS

Question 13:

What features distinguish Network ACLs from security groups within a VPC? (Select three)

A. ACL filters at the subnet level

B. ACL is based on deny rules only

C. ACL is applied to instances and subnets

D. ACL is stateless

E. ACL supports a numbered list for filtering

Question 14:

What two statements correctly describe Auto-Scaling groups?

A. horizontal scaling of capacity

B. decrease number of instances only

C. EC2 instances are assigned to a group

D. database instances only

E. does not support Elastic Load Balancing

F. no support for multiple availability zones

Question 15:

You have been asked to setup a VPC endpoint connection between VPC and S3 buckets for storing backups and snapshots. What AWS component is currently required when configuring a VPC endpoint?

A. Internet gateway

B. NAT instance

C. Elastic IP

D. private IP address

E. Direct Connect

Question 16:

What are two primary advantages of DynamoDB?

A. SQL support

B. managed service

C. performance

D. CloudFront integration

Question 17:

What DNS attributes are configured when a default VPC is selected?

A. DNS resolution: yes
   DNS hostnames: yes

B. DNS resolution: yes
   DNS hostnames: no

C. DNS resolution: no
   DNS hostnames: yes

D. DNS resolution: no
   DNS hostnames: no

Question 18:

What are three primary characteristics of DynamoDB?

A. less scalable than RDS

B. static content

C. store metadata for S3 objects

D. auto-replication to three Availability Zones

E. high read/write throughput

Question 19:

What Amazon AWS service supports real-time processing of data stream from multiple consumers and replay of records?

A. DynamoDB

B. EMR

C. Kinesis data streams

D. SQS

E. RedShift

Question 20:

What are three primary reasons for deploying ElastiCache?

A. data security

B. managed service

C. Redis replication

D. durability

E. low latency

Question 21:

Select three requirements for configuring a Bastion host?

A. EIP

B. SSH inbound permission

C. default route

D. CloudWatch logs group

E. VPN

F. Auto-Scaling

Question 22:

What two features of an API Gateway minimize the effects of peak traffic events and minimize latency?

A. load balancing

B. firewalling

C. throttling

D. scaling

E. caching

Question 23:

What three characteristics differentiate Lambda from traditional EC2 deployment or containerization?

A. Lambda is based on Kinesis scripts

B. Lambda is serverless

C. tenant has ownership of EC2 instances

D. tenant has no control of EC2 instances

E. Lambda is a code-based service

F. Lambda supports only S3 and Glacier

Question 24:

What CIDR block range is supported for IPv4 addressing and subnetting within a single VPC?

A. /16 to /32

B. /16 to /24

C. /16 to /28

D. /16 to /20

Question 25:

What is the default behavior when adding a new subnet to a VPC? (Select two)

A. new subnet is associated with the main route table

B. new subnet is associated with the custom route table

C. new subnet is associated with any selected route table

D. new subnet is assigned to the default subnet

E. new subnet is assigned from the VPC CIDR block

Question 26:

You have enabled Amazon RDS database services in VPC1 for an application that has public web servers in VPC2. How do you connect the web servers to the RDS database instance so they can communicate considering the VPC's are in the same region?

A. VPC endpoints

B. VPN gateway

C. path-based routing

D. VPC peering

E. AWS Network Load Balancer

Question 27:

What are three methods of accessing DynamoDB for customization purposes?

A. CLI

B. AWS console

C. API programmatic call

D. vCenter

E. Beanstalk

Question 28:

What two attributes distinguish each pricing model?

A. reliability

B. amazon service

C. discount

D. performance

E. redundancy

Question 29:

What are two primary differences between Glacier and S3 storage services?

A. Glacier is lower cost

B. S3 is lower cost

C. Glacier is preferred for frequent data access with lower latency

D. S3 is preferred for frequent data access with lower latency

E. S3 supports larger file size

Question 30:

What are three primary **differences** between S3 vs EBS?

A. S3 is a multi-purpose public internet-based storage

B. EBS is directly assigned to a tenant VPC EC2 instance

C. EBS and S3 provide persistent storage

D. EBS snapshots are typically stored on S3 buckets

E. EBS and S3 use buckets to manage files

F. EBS and S3 are based on block level storage

Question 31:

What two statements correctly describe how to add or modify IAM roles to a running EC2 instance?

A. attach an IAM role to an existing EC2 instance from the EC2 console

B. replace an IAM role attached to an existing EC2 instance from the EC2 console

C. attach an IAM role to the user account and relaunch the EC2 instance

D. add the EC2 instance to a group where the role is a member

Question 32:

When is Direct Connect a preferred solution over VPN IPsec?

A. fast and reliable connection

B. redundancy is a key requirement

C. fast and easy to deploy

D. layer 3 connectivity

E. layer 2 connectivity

Question 33:

What two features correctly describe an Application Load Balancer (ALB)?

A. dynamic port mapping

B. SSL listener

C. layer 7 load balancer

D. backend server authentication

E. multi-region forwarding

Question 34:

What AWS storage solution allows thousands of EC2 instances to simultaneously upload, access, delete and share files?

A. EBS

B. S3

C. Glacier

D. EFS

E. Storage Gateway

Question 35:

Select two custom origin servers from the following?

A. S3 bucket

B. S3 object

C. EC2 instance

D. elastic load balancer

E. API gateway

Question 36:

How do you launch an EC2 instance after it is terminated? (Select two)

A. launch a new instance using the same AMI

B. reboot instance from CLI

C. launch a new instance from a Snapshot

D. reboot instance from management console

E. contact AWS support to reset

Question 37:

You recently made some configuration changes to an EC2 instance. You then launched a new EC2 instance from the same AMI however none of the settings were saved. What is the cause of this error?

A. did not save configuration changes to EC2 instance

B. did not save configuration changes to AMI

C. did not create new AMI

D. did not reboot EC2 instance to enable changes

Question 38:

What are two primary difference between Amazon S3 Standard and S3/RRS storage classes?

A. Amazon Standard does not replicate at all

B. RRS provides higher durability

C. RRS provides higher availability

D. RRS does not replicate objects as many times

E. application usage is different

Question 39:

What is required to Ping from a source instance to a destination instance?

A. Network ACL: not required
   Security Group: allow ICMP outbound on source/destination EC2 instances

B. Network ACL: allow ICMP inbound/outbound on source/destination subnets
   Security Group: not required

C. Network ACL: allow ICMP inbound/outbound on source/destination subnets
   Security Group: allow ICMP outbound on source EC2 instance
   Security Group: allow ICMP inbound on destination EC2 instance

D. Network ACL: allow TCP inbound/outbound on source/destination subnets
   Security Group: allow TCP and ICMP inbound on source EC2 instance

Question 40:

What is the recommended method for migrating (copying) an EC2 instance to a different region?

A. terminate instance, select region, copy instance to destination region

B. select AMI associated with EC2 instance and use *Copy AMI* option

C. stop instance and copy AMI to destination region

D. cross-region copy is not currently supported

Question 41:

What service can automate EBS snapshots (backups) for restoring EBS volumes?

A. CloudWatch event

B. SNS topic

C. CloudTrail

D. Amazon Inspector

E. CloudWatch alarm

Question 42:

What is required to copy an encrypted EBS snapshot cross-account? (Select two)

A. copy the unencrypted EBS snapshot to an S3 bucket

B. distribute the custom key from CloudFront

C. share the custom key for the snapshot with the target account

D. share the encrypted EBS snapshot with the target account

E. share the encrypted EBS snapshots publicly

F. enable root access security on both accounts

Question 43:

How are snapshots for an EBS volume created when it is the root device for an instance?

A. pause instance, unmount volume and snapshot

B. terminate instance and snapshot

C. unencrypt volume and snapshot dynamically

D. stop instance, unmount volume and snapshot

Question 44:

How are packets forwarded between public and private subnets within a VPC?

A. EIP

B. NAT

C. main route table

D. VPN

Question 45:

What statements correctly describe security groups within a VPC? (Select three)

A. default security group only permit inbound traffic

B. security groups are stateful firewalls

C. only allow rules are supported

D. allow and deny rules are supported

E. security groups are associated to network interfaces

Question 46:

How is routing enabled by default within a VPC for an EC2 instance?

A. add a default route

B. main route table

C. custom route table

D. must be configured explicitly

Question 47:

What is typically associated with Microservices? (Select two)

A. ALB

B. Kinesis

C. RDS

D. DynamoDB

E. ECS

F. EFS

Question 48:

What is the advantage of read-after-write consistency for S3 buckets?

A. no stale reads for PUT of any new object in all regions

B. higher throughput for all requests

C. stale reads for PUT requests in some regions

D. no stale reads for GET requests in a single regions

Question 49:

What two statements correctly describe versioning for protecting data at rest on S3 buckets?

A. enabled by default

B. creates snapshots

C. overwrites most current file version

D. restores deleted files

E. saves multiple versions of a single file

F. disabled by default

Question 50:

What attributes are selectable when creating an EBS volume for an EC2 instance? (Select three)

A. volume type

B. IOPS

C. region

D. CMK

E. EIP

Question 51:

How does AWS uniquely identify S3 objects?

A. bucket name

B. version

C. key

D. object tag

Question 52:

You have been asked to migrate a 10 GB unencrypted EBS volume to an encrypted volume for security purposes. What are three key steps required as part of the migration?

A. pause the unencrypted instance

B. create a new encrypted volume of the same size and availability zone

C. create a new encrypted volume of the same size in any availability zone

D. start converter instance

E. shutdown and detach the unencrypted instance

Question 53:

How is an EBS root volume created when launching an EC2 instance from a new EBS-backed AMI?

A. S3 template

B. original AMI

C. Snapshot

D. instance store

Question 54:

What is an EBS Snapshot? (select the best answer)

A. backup of an EBS root volume and instance data

B. backup of an EC2 instance

C. backup of configuration settings

D. backup of instance store

Question 55:

What feature is supported when attaching or detaching an EBS volume from an EC2 instance?

A. any available EBS volume can be attached and detached to an EC2 instance in the same region

B. any available EBS volume can be attached and detached to an EC2 instance that is cross-region

C. any available EBS volume can only be copied and attached to an EC2 instance that is cross-region

D. any available EBS volume can only be attached and detached to an EC2 instance in the same Availability Zone

Question 56:

How is a volume selected (identified) when making an EBS Snapshot?

A. account id

B. volume id

C. tag

D. ARN

Question 57:

What is a requirement for attaching VPC EC2 instances to on-premises clients?

A. Amazon Virtual private gateway (VPN)

B. Amazon Internet Gateway

C. VPN Connection

D. Elastic Load Balancer (ELB)

E. NAT

Question 58:

What three features are characteristic of Classic Load Balancers?

A. dynamic port mapping

B. path-based routing

C. SSL listener

D. backend server authentication

E. ECS

F. Layer 4 based load balancer

Question 59:

What consistency model is the default used by DynamoDB?

A. strongly consistent

B. eventually consistent

C. no default model

D. casual consistency

E. sequential consistency

Question 60:

What encryption support is available for tenants that are deploying AWS DynamoDB?

A. server-side encryption

B. client-side encryption

C. client-side and server-side encryption

D. encryption not supported

E. block level encryption

Answer Key

1. A,D,E
2. B,C
3. A
4. D
5. A
6. A,C,D
7. D
8. B,E
9. C,D,E
10. A,C,E
11. A,B
12. D
13. A,D,E
14. A,C
15. D
16. B,C
17. A
18. C,D,E
19. C
20. B,C,E
21. A,B,D
22. C,E
23. B,D,E
24. C
25. A,E
26. D
27. A,B,C
28. A,C
29. A,D

30. A,B,D

31. A,B

32. A

33. A,C

34. D

35. C,D

36. A,C

37. C

38. D,E

39. C

40. B

41. A

42. C,D

43. D

44. B

45. B,C,E

46. B

47. A,E

48. A

49. D,F

50. A,B,D

51. C

52. B,D,E

53. C

54. A

55. D

56. D

57. B

58. C,D,F

59. B

60. B

Amazon Publications

The following are some additional study tools comprised of books, practice tests and labs. Request a free tier account from Amazon AWS and get practical experience with creating EC2 instances, S3 buckets, IAM, file backups and VPC configuration.

Amazon Books

- AWS Certified Solutions Architect Associate Practice Questions
- Cloud Computing: Architecture Fundamentals for Cloud Systems

Practice Tests

https://www.udemy.com/aws-certified-solutions-architect-associate-exam-extended/

AWS Publications

AWS Labs
https://aws.amazon.com/training/intro-to-aws-labs-sm/

AWS Labs
https://aws.amazon.com/getting-started/labs/

10-Minute Tutorials
https://aws.amazon.com/getting-started/tutorials/

Amazon AWS White Papers
https://aws.amazon.com/whitepapers/

Amazon AWS FAQs
https://aws.amazon.com/faqs/

33116490R00097

Made in the USA
Middletown, DE
11 January 2019